$1 50

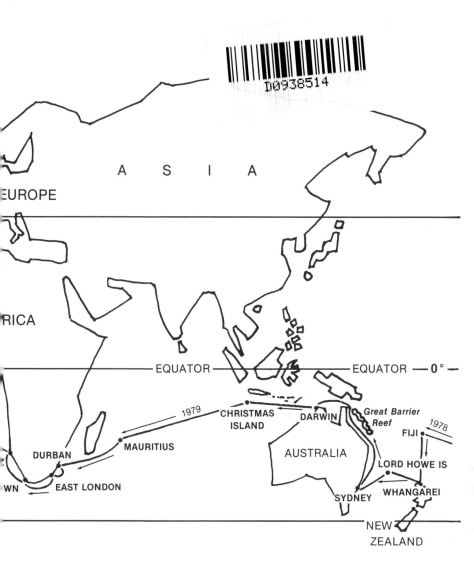

D0938514

A S I A

EUROPE

RICA

EQUATOR

EQUATOR — 0° —

1979

CHRISTMAS
ISLAND

DARWIN

Great Barrier
Reef

FIJI

1978

DURBAN

MAURITIUS

AUSTRALIA

LORD HOWE IS

WN

EAST LONDON

SYDNEY

WHANGAREI

NEW
ZEALAND

*By
Way
of the
Wind*

Swan *in a painting by Kirk Barnes.*

By Way of the Wind

JIM MOORE

SHERIDAN HOUSE

To Molly, my wife, my first mate, my support.
If, during this walk through the years, for a few
fleeting moments I soared with the eagles, it was,
because, you were the wind beneath my wings.

ACKNOWLEDGEMENTS
I would like to thank Kirk and Gladys Barnes for their helpful
comments and proofreading of the manuscript, and for their
encouragement during this writing effort.

Library of Congress Cataloging-in-Publication Data
Moore, Jim, 1936-
    By way of the wind / Jim Moore.
        p.   cm.
    ISBN 0-924486-09-0
    1. Swan (Sailboat) 2. Swan (Sailboat) 3. Voyages around the
world— 1981- I. Title.
G440.S95M66 1991
910.4'1—dc20   90-49484
                                                          CIP

Cover and design by Jeremiah B. Lighter
Printed in the United States of America
ISBN 0-924486-09-0

1

"WE'RE GOING to build a boat and sail it to the South Pacific!" I blurted this out to my bride of two months as I burst through the door of the houseboat. She stared blankly at me. "We can quit these lousy jobs and do something exciting for once!"

She stood there stirring the chili. "Did you remember to pick up the onions?"

I could see that she was warming to the idea.

It was June 1972. For many weeks we had considered all sorts of ideas of something adventuresome to do with our lives. We were both 36 years old, had been in our respective jobs in Portland, Oregon for about 10 years, and were totally aghast at the idea of maintaining the status quo for the next couple of decades. We were looking for a change. It was now or never—I was certain of that.

My current excitement stemmed from a small ad in the paper placed by Yacht Constructors, a local boatbuilder. They would deliver any of their three sizes of boat—the Cascade 29, 36, or 42—in any stage of completion. I had visited their factory earlier and had already picked the boat for us. We were middle income, middle class, middle everything, so the 36 was it. The fact that neither Molly nor I had ever set foot on a sailboat, or had the slightest inkling of how to build or sail one, never bothered me whatsoever—something I still wonder about.

I heard that a Cascade 42 had just arrived at the harbor and I wanted to have a look at it. Perhaps it would help get Molly into the swing of things. I sweetened the deal by suggesting that we put the chili on hold, have a look at the boat, then go out for beer and Mexican food—play some shuffleboard. This was a trump card that I played only on rare occasions. She agreed.

I was on a roll. The skipper and his wife invited us aboard. He had completed most of the boat's construction and it was a workmanlike job. Any doubts I'd harbored about my own ability to do a similar job were erased when he informed me that he was a commercial airline pilot and not a carpenter or shipwright. His wife was showing Molly the galley and giving her little tips, and it all seemed to be gelling. When they told us they had just sailed back from Tahiti we were glued to their every word. There was no doubt. We would build a boat and sail it to the South Pacific—after a few details had been worked out.

During the building period, which was to encompass four years, several fortuitous things happened. First, we located a place to build the boat. At that time we were living in a houseboat on the Columbia River. We enjoyed the lifestyle and were reluctant to change it. As luck would have it, a large boathouse (different from a houseboat in that a boat is the principal tenant) came up for sale the very week we ordered the hull. We bought it on the spot. After some renovation, we had a small studio apartment at the front, and a covered boat well at the rear with ample room to work on the boat. There were areas on each side of the well to set up power tools, and it suited us fine. We would be living just a few feet from our floating baby.

One of the great blessings in life is that one cannot foresee the future. If the reverse were possible, I am reasonably sure that most boatbuilding projects would not get beyond the dream stage. It seemed that our every waking hour revolved around the boat. It influenced nearly everything we did. Any purchases that we made were weighed against future use and storage problems on board. On our first wedding anniversary I bought "us" a gift of a tap and die set with matching drill bits. Molly was all choked up and didn't speak for hours.

In the spring of 1973 we were in Westerlund's boatyard, about to fit a 4333-pound keel to our 36-foot fiberglass hull, or rather fit the hull to the keel. (One doesn't do much moving of keels.) The keel fit into an indentation in the hull, and pre-drilled holes were supposed to line up on centers with large athwartship beams that ace boatbuilder and wife had fiberglassed into place earlier.

I was bordering on paranoia at the thought of drilling the holes through the hull until I knew for certain that everything was in alignment. After a great deal of measuring I was still reluctant to drill. Suddenly it occurred to me that sunlight cast shadows of the beams through the hull, and for a brief period each day the sun was exactly 90 degrees to the centerline of the boat. At that point the shadows of the beams would not be distorted. It is understandable that this solution took a little time manifesting itself, as I had lived in Oregon for fifteen years and the sun, with its rare appearances, doesn't play much of a part in life there. I think that Oregonians are one of the few groups of Americans that could live through a nuclear winter without realizing it had occurred.

But it was June and luck was with us. When the sun was making a meridian passage vis-à-vis the beams, I banged on the hull and Molly marked their exact position. We drilled the holes dead-center. That was the first of a long period of guidance that the sun would provide for us.

We fitted the major bulkheads in place before the

boat was lowered into the water so the hull would retain its exact design shape. As the cables lifting our brand new boat took a strain, raising her high above the dock, and she began the descent toward the water, all laws of physics and marine design flew out the window. Deep down I knew that I had been a part of all of this, and could somehow have altered the balance of forces. All I could see was that the huge hunk of metal hanging on the bottom of the boat was intent on dragging baby straight down to the bottom the moment they took the slings off. But when she entered the water the crane operator never even slowed down. The slings dropped away and she sat there floating six inches higher than her scribed waterline, empty as she was. I resolved to put more trust in science and less trust in my phobias.

Now the real work began—four to five hours every night, and every weekend.

Construction began in the bow for two reasons. First, any initial errors that we made would be less glaring, and second, it's fairly straightforward work with very little expensive equipment to install. We needed a financial recovery period after the initial outlays.

By this time we had accumulated a fairly large library of nautical books. I read every boatbuilding book I could find and tried to incorporate the best of their contents into our boat. On the kitchen wall hung a large map of the South Pacific, which we had wisely covered with plastic. Our proposed route, marked on it with grease pencil, was changed about a dozen times.

Molly was, by now, fully engrossed in our new life and plans. She was sporting a "First Mate" sweatshirt and picking up the jargon, or most of it. She would be showing guests the progress of the boat, and at times would refer to the bow as "the pointed end," which had a way of detracting from her "born in the fo'c'sle" image.

There is no short supply of visitors to a boat in the process of construction. For the most part I enjoyed these visits, except for a few individuals who had a modicum of sailing experience and knew that I had none. They felt that this gave them special license to give me lectures on the perils of the sea and the difficulties involved in becoming a competent sailor. I would sometimes cool them off by responding, "Wow, I didn't know there were big waves and everything out there!"

Learning to sail was by far the easiest obstacle to overcome during the preparation years. Some years later, in Durban, South Africa, I asked four experienced cruising sailors what was the biggest obstacle they had to overcome during their building periods and voyages. Money was the one-word answer. I assumed they meant the lack of it.

Days, weeks, and months ran together, and at last we were ready to fit the deck in place. Yacht Constructors builds a first-class deck unit of molded fiberglass lined with marine plywood. I rented a truck and trailer and by some miracle managed to get the deck to Westerlund's yard in one piece. My optimism was somewhat daunted when I was nearly killed by the crane that was to lift the deck. A piece of steel had work-hardened and parted, dropping a large steel ring about eighty feet. It smashed through the trailer bed three feet from where I was standing. Thoroughly shaken, I opted to be a bystander as the crane lowered the deck onto the boat.

I had cut the bulkheads about one inch high for fitting later, and the deck sat unevenly on them. Two months were consumed trimming bulkheads, jacking the deck up and down, endlessly checking that everything fit exactly right. In August of 1975 we fastened hull and deck with resorcinol glue, bronze boat nails, screws, and through-bolts. We then faired the hull/deck joint and applied six layers of fiberglass cloth for strength and watertight integrity. In the course of sailing 40,000 nautical miles, often in gales and bashing seas, not one drop of water has entered the boat through a seam or fitting (knock on fiberglass).

We were now more than two years into building the boat and it still didn't have a name. We wanted to name her something that wasn't cutesy, or so esoteric that it required a lengthy explanation. We had exhausted the classics and the whole subject had exhausted me, but not Molly. She never wavered for a moment. The phone would ring where I worked and I would pick up the receiver. A voice would say, "Isle of Dreams"—Bam! Then one day we let baby out of the boat house on a tether, and her white hull was mirrored in the water. Molly said it looked like a swan sitting there. *Swan!* Sierra-Whiskey-Alfa-November—clean and simple.

In the early summer of 1976 we began rigging *Swan*. The mast was laid out along the walkway, and as I worked there was no dearth of advice from the passersby. I took great care in running the electrical wires through the mast, spiralling them around a supporting line and keeping it all in the center of the mast with foam rubber blocks attached every three feet. I ran double sail tracks for the main and storm trysail, a feature that we were thankful for many times during the voyage.

For three years I had been cooped up in the shed and my poolroom pallor was impressive even by Oregon standards. It was great working outside, and some color was returning. We had a goal. We wanted to sail the maiden voyage on July 4, 1976, the United States Bicentennial.

On the afternoon of the fourth, last-minute preparations were taking place. The mast stood straight and tall, the sails were in place, the big moment had arrived. A huge fireworks display was planned by the city of Vancouver, Washington for that evening, and hundreds of boats were anchored to view the spectacle. This eliminated the usual crush of boats sailing about the river, and would also make any blunders we might make less public. A turn of the key and *Swan*'s 25-hp. two-banger Volvo diesel engine sprang to life. We slipped the lines with some trepidation and motored into the channel.

About a half-mile into this landmark voyage the engine missed a couple of beats and died. No sails were up and I'm not sure what I would have done with them anyway, since there wasn't any wind in this sheltered channel. The engine refused to fire and we were rapidly being set down by the current towards an ugly bunch of pilings.

Jimminy Cricket repeatedly pounded into Pinocchio's head that you can learn almost anything from books. Jimminy's lesson was not lost on me. The sailing books said to have an anchor free for running when entering or leaving port. Our dock was the port and our anchor was ready to run. In a few seconds the 35-pound CQR anchor and all-chain rode was rattling over the bow roller. It dug in, *Swan*'s bow swung smartly into the current, and she stopped a short distance from the pilings.

The fireworks were beginning by the time I had corrected the problem. During the process of bleeding the air out of the fuel system I had neglected to tighten a fitting and air had entered the system. Diesels don't like that.

Underway again and feeling pretty good about the way we had handled our first little emergency we motored out of the channel into the river. A brisk northwest wind was blowing and the mate was on the foredeck. In a booming voice I said, "Haul up the main!" A perplexed expression was on the mate's face. "The starboard winch!" I shouted into the wind. "I don't care which way you're facing—starboard is still starboard! It's on the Oregon side of the boat!"

With the main and reacher up *Swan* shot ahead. This startled me. I'm not sure what I expected to happen. She would have shot ahead a little faster had it not been for a three-year-old marine garden growing on the undersides. In the distance the rockets volleyed and thundered. It was all rather grand.

ONE MORNING a friend telephoned and informed us that a mutual friend had died. This carried double impact for me. First, a good man had passed on, and second, he was a refrigeration man. Now I don't have a special fixation for refrigeration men, but this particular man expired after I had followed his instructions to the letter, installing refrigeration equipment in every nook and cranny of the engine compartment. He was supposed to hook all of it together.

Until then my knowledge of refrigeration was that it was cold and good for beer. Now I was forced to buy a big thick book on refrigeration and educate myself on the theory and mechanics of refrigeration, no doubt with Jimminy C's approval. It all turned out for the best—now I could do for myself the one piece of work on the boat, other than welding, that I had originally intended to have done by someone else.

A footnote on this subject is that the system never failed during the voyage of nearly four years, and as I write this book it still hasn't failed after 10 years of near-continuous use. This, I can assure you, is very rare for a marine refrigeration system.

The overworked debate over whether a cruising yacht needs refrigeration on board tires me. We personally found that it made life on board much more civilized, and we wouldn't be without it. Sometimes a would-be cruiser asks me, in a slightly argumentative tone, "Do you really need refrigeration?" I ask them if they have a refrigerator at home. When they say yes, I ask them, "Do you use it?"

Spring of 1977 was at hand. The boathouse was up for sale. September 10, 1977 was D-Day. Four months left, with much to be done. We installed a low-silhouette cockpit dodger and a wind-operated self-steering vane—two indispensable items on a cruising yacht. We strung jacklines fore and aft on the side decks. Short tethers with plastic thimbles slipped over the jacklines, and were equipped with carabiner hooks for clipping to a safety harness. The tether would slide along the lines like a dog's leash on a clothesline.

We decided to wear safety harnesses at all times on deck at sea, good weather or bad. We have strong feelings on this subject. A cruising couple we knew were on an ocean passage and the woman was on watch, apparently not wearing a safety harness. Later, her husband came on deck and she had vanished. The search was futile. The horror of watching your world sail over the horizon without you is the stuff of nightmares. It was not going to become a reality on our voyage.

We planned to leave on September 10 and we worked up to and including the ninth, as hard as that is to believe. We were going in one great quantum leap from total work to total play, although some of the impending "play" could well be seen otherwise.

The evening of the tenth was a Friday and the boys at General Motors, where I worked, threw a big wingding for us. I vaguely remember coming home in the wee hours. It was our last night in the boathouse. We'd sold it to our neighbors for a nice profit, and they allowed us to live there until D-Day. "Just leave the keys on the table." Good folks.

At 0500 the alarm jangled, sending great jabs of raw pain through my brain. On my first day of freedom I lay there in the throes of a terminal hangover. The telephone rang, compounding my agony. It was one of my degenerate friends, still out on the rampage, calling to tell me that he had checked the morning paper, that we were not in the obituaries, and were therefore free to leave. The mate was in disgustingly good shape.

I am fairly certain that *Swan* would have been completed far earlier had it not been for a few of my friends, one in particular being Darold Brown. Darold and his wife, our dear friend Linda, moored their sailboat behind our boathouse. Darold and I, both slightly intemperate Irishmen, often worked on technical problems of construction together. During these sessions we often focused on the problem through the bottom of a wineglass. These research and development periods usually ended in much laughing and carrying-on. Scratch another late night of work. It was all great fun.

Our neighbors heard *Swan*'s engine start and some of them came out to take pictures of our departure. The flashbulbs and diesel smell combined to push me nearer to the brink of death. My one desire in life was to get the boat a few miles downriver, away from the threat of an impromptu party, drop the hook, and get my act together. The mate was bubbly and all smiles, enjoying every minute of the attention. I could have flogged her on the spot.

Nightfall found us 60 miles downstream, anchored on the Washington side of the river. The pure excitement of leaving had worked miracles in the skipper's recovery.

The following afternoon we made our way into a transient berth at West Basin Marina in Astoria, Oregon. The water was part salt and part fresh; the fat was in the fire.

It was a grayish misty morning when *Swan* nosed out into the ebbing tide and onto the Columbia River Bar. That was when the full impact of our decision came down on me. Security is a big word. We had grown accustomed to the benefits of a large corporation. Any problems would now fall squarely on our shoulders. We had put together a cruising budget, but it was just that. A time would come when we would have to deal with the future. But not now. What was it that old Harry Truman said about standing the heat in the kitchen? We were now 41 years old and we were reaching for the brass ring. I have never regretted our decision to break away for an instant.

Our final send-off took place off the Oregon coast. Two of our friends were pilots and they loaded up their planes with our raucous pals and gave us a hero's send-off, complete with rolls of toilet paper streaming down. All of this festive stuff coincided with Molly's first bout with seasickness. Fortunately hers was usually short-lived.

Swan marked off the miles. Her first encounter with ocean conditions and she was handling them like a veteran. The steering vane wasn't. A beam wind should have been duck soup for the vane, but something wasn't right—we were all over the ocean. While Molly steered, I spent several hours hanging over the pushpit adjusting things until my chest was sore as a boil. If the boat came up on the wind the vane worked better; if it fell off and the apparent wind decreased, it wouldn't work at all. It was clear that more wind was required to operate it than was reasonable. Darkness fell and I gave up on the problem. We would steer watch on, watch off, one hour each.

The steering problems were temporarily put to rest when the wind faded and died with the coming of night and was replaced by a cold damp fog, about the worst thing I could think of for our first night at sea—wallowing in the trough with a seasick mate, in limited visibility, smack in the middle of the shipping lanes.

It soon became apparent that I harbored a deeper concern than I had realized about being on a boat in proximity of land at night. I still do, and for a very good reason: Land is what sinks most boats, because rock is harder than water.

The depth sounder alarm beeped when triggered by a fish. This would startle me, and I would stare anxiously toward land into the murk and the gloom. My active imagination had long ago conjured up a vivid picture of *Swan* being dashed to bits on the rocks.

I dropped the jib and started the engine, steering a southwesterly course. It was a Catch 22: With the engine running we couldn't hear an approaching ship; with it off we couldn't move out of harm's way. But at least now we had a chance to run out of the fog and perhaps find some of those long ocean swells I had read so much about.

Molly looked like a stuffed orange bear with all the clothing she was wearing under her foul weather gear. Being on deck was better for her *mal de mer*, but a following zephyr blew diesel fumes into the cockpit to her great annoyance. My offhand remark, "At least I'm not popping flashbulbs at you," drew a withering glare and a protracted silence. She sat in the corner of the cockpit, staring into the fog.

We muddled through the night, and with dawn the southerly wind returned, sweeping away most of the fog. Anticipating the possibility of seasickness, Molly had prepared a few meals in advance and put them in the refrigerator. She wasn't in the mood to eat, but I was famished. I went below and wolfed down a couple bowls of stew in preparation for my assault on the wind vane.

After reading and rereading the owner's manual, I fastened a boat cushion on the railing to protect my sore chest and studied the problem. The two parallel control cables leading down to the rudder servo were, by the book, exactly five inches apart at a prescribed point. I had checked this numerous times. As I studied the action it appeared to be sluggish for some reason. I spread the cables just slightly, which increased the tension, and the vane seized up noticeably. I was onto something! I loosened the cable turnbuckles, gave the system another inch of slack, and the vane was born again! The balancing counterweight moved smartly with each nuance of boat movement and steered *Swan* as if she were on railroad tracks. The mate was only too glad to tie the helm amidships and allow the vane to take over.

The sea was filled with white horses, the wind was at Force 5 and increasing. With all the starts, stops, and distractions I had little faith in my DR (dead reckoning) position and there was no chance for a celestial fix. We wanted to put in at Coos Bay, Oregon for reasons that now elude me. Finally I jabbed my finger down at a spot about forty miles offshore and announced: "We're off the Oregon coast right about here." An "oh, great" came from the cockpit. If we were near the EP (estimated position) we might fetch Coos Bay on one tack.

Ready about! Put the vane in neutral. Hard a-lee! Through the eye of the wind she comes—the sail backs. Headlong into the trough—green water crashes on deck. *Swan*'s first real blue water, rough-sea work. No wearing ship for this lady! Harden the working sheet and she hauls off on the starboard tack.

If the EP were anywhere near correct, an unknown that was now prefacing nearly every tactical thought I had, we should arrive around noon. At dawn visibility was no more than 300 yards and we had fired up the iron spinnaker again in an attempt to point higher and charge the systems. (We were using electricity as if we owned the Hoover Dam.) The depth sounder found the bottom at 60 fathoms and I was hoping to obtain a sun line to cross with the 50-fathom curve on the chart to fix our position. No chance, nor at 40 fathoms either. I considered turning south and motoring along the 40-fathom curve using the depth sounder. It would not fix our position in and of itself, but it would at least guarantee that we were running south at a safe distance offshore on a line somewhere between Alaska and San Diego. I chose to keep this little gem of navigation from the mate.

We pressed on, glued to the depth sounder, and then, fortunately, the weather began to clear. In the distance we could see what appeared to be breakwaters. After taking bow-on bearings on every salient point I attempted to construct a pattern on the chart.

I never trusted bearings taken on mountains that were part of a range because I could rarely identify them. The sailing directions and coast pilots would say something like this: "Viewed at bearing 224 true, 6.5 to 7 miles distant, High Butte Crag resembles the left profile of a female walrus." Even British Admiralty charts with those excellent profile sketches of the land never beguiled me into trusting my ability to discern, with absolute certainty, that the mountain in the hazy distance was, in fact, the one that looked so obvious on the chart.

As the distance closed I was sure it was Coos Bay. A fishing trawler was coming towards us about two points on the starboard bow. I turned toward them, which increased the pounding considerably, and when we came within hailing distance I swallowed my pride and shouted, "Is that Coos Bay?" They returned a thumbs up. I had been trying to figure a way of finding out from them if it was Coos Bay without resorting to asking them point-blank. But then I noticed that they were wearing overalls and red checkered shirts, and I had lived in Oregon long enough to know that you don't try to con Oregonians who dressed like that.

This momentary blow to my ego was quickly overshadowed by the realization that we had, indeed, sailed some 90 miles out to someplace and back in the worst of conditions and had hit Coos Bay dead on. The mate was impressed. I was speechless.

Our stop at Coos Bay has been an enduring source of amazement. At that point we were victims of the beginning cruiser's syndrome—a pervading sense that cruising meant moving, not sitting at the dock. It was as if someone were grading our performance. Here we were in a nice quiet marina with a restaurant, bar, showers, laundry, and comfort. But did we wait for a nice northerly? Did we check out the town, cook an elaborate meal, enjoy the rest? Not us. We left the following morning on the same adverse wind, close-hauled on the port tack on the old familiar southwesterly course, thrashing and bashing our heads against the wall. We had a lot to learn.

Off the coast of northern California the weather deteriorated further. The fickle sun disappeared and soon we were in the middle of a full-blown gale. The mainsail was securely down, and in its place was the spanking new storm trysail. It and the working jib were driving hard—too hard for my liking. At times *Swan* would fly off the crest of a wave; a jaw-clenching moment of suspended animation would follow, and she would hit with a bone-jarring jolt that made me wonder why the keel didn't continue on straight to the bottom. The water was relatively shallow, which helped create short-period steep seas, an uncomfortable and potentially dangerous combination.

Reducing sail had been on my mind for an hour or so, which was in direct violation of the rule that if, at sea, you are even considering reducing sail, you should. Foam was blowing off the crests of the waves and it was becoming a constant fight to avoid rounding up. I wasn't looking forward to life on the foredeck, but there wasn't much choice in the matter. About this time the orange bear came on deck and made what must be, in retrospect, one of the greatest understatements in cruising history. "Maybe we should have stayed in Coos Bay another day."

"Oh no, not us," I roared. "Did you ever hear of lemmings? They migrate with such mindless zeal that they stampede into the ocean and drown! That's us, Jim and Molly Lemming!"

From bear to lemming. The mate was fast going through the menagerie.

Leaving the vane in charge of steering, we went forward tethered to the jacklines. Down came the jib, and it was stuffed into the bag. We raised the heavy storm jib while being pummeled with blasts of cold seawater and scrambled back to the cockpit laughing at the pure outrageousness of it all. The windward work was much more subdued now.

For one brief shining moment we were bathed in sunlight and I managed to get a quick sight. The sun was almost due south, which made the resulting line of position (LOP) run in an east-west direction. This, coupled with the depth sounder readings, gave us a fairly accurate position.

One celestial sight does not establish a fix. The LOP tells you that the ship is on a line but not exactly *where* on that line. The second sight, either with another celestial body or the same body after it has had time to make an apparent move, provides another LOP which the ship is also on. If the ship is on two lines at once it can *only* be where they cross; hence the fix. If you are standing on Hollywood and Vine, simultaneously, you have to be in the middle of that intersection. Got it!

If you are interested in learning celestial navigation, which isn't all that difficult, forget all of that stuff your high school teacher told you about the planet earth being an insignificant speck in the galaxy. Copernicus was wrong. The earth is, and I wouldn't steer you wrong, the absolute center of the Milky Way and probably the universe, and all heavenly bodies revolve around us. The people who wrote the Nautical Almanac know this. They don't cloud the facts by suggesting the earth revolves. They say the sun rises and the sun sets, pure and simple. It goes around to the other side and shines where the Chinese live and then comes back around to us. It's a simple and fair system, and if you study the art of celestial navigation I strongly suggest that you look at it in this manner. Besides, it makes you feel much more important.

The wind showed no signs of abating and the seas were worked up to the point that we were frightened by them. The bashing was taking its toll on us and we were utterly fatigued. Simple mental problems like converting magnetic bearings to true now had to be done on paper. We were making so much leeway that it all seemed pointless. I taxed my tired brain to the utmost and mentally ran through the five alternatives for sailboats in storms offshore:

—press on under sail
—heave to under sail
—lie ahull
—ride to a sea anchor
—scud, or run off

The pressing on thing was wearing thin, and heaving to under sail was the only other tactic on the list that we had practiced. (Lying ahull on the Columbia River would hardly have constituted a learning experience.)

We brought the bow through the eye of the wind without releasing the sheet and the storm jib backed. The mate let out the main boom to decrease the pressure on the trysail. I positioned the helm slightly to leeward to prevent her from falling off when she forereached and presto, we were hove to. It wasn't exactly like being on grandma's veranda but the pounding had stopped. We were heeled over about 12 degrees and there seemed to be no threat of tripping on the keel on the face of the seas. I chose the port tack so the crabbing off would carry us seaward.

The mate was completely over her seasickness and was able to prepare a meal in the relative stability. We were both in good spirits and pleased with the way we were handling the storm. However, I could see a disconcerting pattern developing. We seemed to be getting ourselves into life-threatening situations that might easily have been avoided and then feeling jubilant because we hadn't killed ourselves. Storms are usually unavoidable on long passages, but you don't run out of port looking for them! I planned to give this some serious thought in the future.

Night fell. This automatically makes scary things scarier. The odd sea that was larger than average would loom up against the gray sky, towering over us down in the valley, threatening to engulf us in one great inundation of cold Pacific. At what seemed far too calm an approach for the slack-jawed skipper, *Swan* would feel the surge of the sea and at the last possible moment lift on its face, and the rogue would pass harmlessly beneath us with a great whooshing roar. Given half a chance *Swan* was going to take good care of us.

A powerful coastal navigation light provided us the means to fix our position, and this eased my mind considerably. The mate took the first watch and woke me after what seemed like only a few minutes. I lay there totally disoriented, listening to the commotion of the sea. I had slept three hours but my head was full of cobwebs. The reassuring flash of the navigation light shone through the port.

I stared at the chart for a time, trying to remember why I was looking at it. Molly took over my lee bunk and I snapped on my harness at the companionway and went on deck. I had by no means become inured to the towering rogues, and one or two were sufficient to clear my head of any lingering cobwebs. I took a hand-bearing compass reading on the light and was unable to discern any change, except that we were farther offshore. We appeared to be crabbing off at 90 degrees to the shoreline, which was fine with me.

I set the travel alarm clock for one hour and would advance it before it rang; standard procedure on watch. An hour or so passed as I sat in the protection of the dodger, reading by a small red cockpit light. Occasionally I would check the bearing of the shore light. During one of these checks I scanned the entire horizon, something I should have been doing all along. Peering over the dodger I was horrified to see an enormous barge bearing down on us with two tugs trying to arrest its wind-driven forward motion. I started the engine and left it in neutral. The main was prevented out to leeward, so it dictated the direction to go. Frantically I snapped the jib over and it filled with a bang. We moved smartly ahead. By this time Saucer Eyes was at the companionway, gaping at the behemoth close upon us. *Swan* was bounding along on a reach at an astonishing speed. Safely out of the way of the barge I brought the bow up and hove-to on the port tack. My heart was hammering as I stood there in the pelting spray watching the tug's losing battle with the barge. The rest of the night was spent over-checking the horizon.

About the time we were resigning ourselves to being hove-to as a way of life, the tiger wind began to lose its teeth. It was like a kitten at 25 knots and we got underway. The storm jib was replaced by the working jib after the customary circus on the foredeck, as a large sea was still running. After three days of frustrating winds and tiresome motoring we raised the Farallon Islands off the coast at San Francisco.

Sailing under the Golden Gate Bridge was an event of high emotion for us. There was at once a feeling a pride in having completed our first passage—an arduous and often frightening one—and a thankfulness that we had managed to come through it unscathed.

One way we didn't come through it was dry! Nearly every stitch of outer clothing we owned was sodden with salt water. We had committed the novice's blunder of transferring salt residue to the cushions below, and they were perpetually damp from moisture absorption. Every cushion cover and environmental surface was washed until *Swan* was pronounced sodium free. That was the last time we made that mistake.

All of this busy work didn't prevent me from staging an occasional foray into the Golden Gate Yacht Club bar. There I assumed the air of the seasoned salt. "Routine passage," I assured the regulars. "Caught in a little blow off Crescent City."

The San Francisco stop made us realize that our new lifestyle was going to entail a lot of walking. From this point of view small towns suit the cruising life better than large ones. The ever-present reality that our cruising budget was by no means a bottomless pit put taxis out of the picture during the voyage for the most part, except in those countries where the dollar exchange allowed this luxury. Our Portland dollar didn't enjoy a favorable exchange rate in San Francisco, so we provisioned for the next leg of the voyage by city bus and on foot.

Our thoughts were on the passage at hand. Our marriage had survived the first leg, and surprisingly our ordeal in the storm had not dampened our enthusiasm to carry on. On that encouraging note, *and* with a favorable weather forecast, we sailed into the blue Pacific, bound for Hilo, Hawaii. It was October 1, 1977.

3

O PEN OCEAN. Moving well under main and jib in a
fair northwest wind. Pelicans everywhere. "Pelican,
pelican, your bill can hold more than your belly
can," I whimsically entered in the log. Two years later,
an Australian girl looked up from reading our log and
said, "Like hell it can. Just finishing one of your entries."

I was so excited I could scarcely contain myself.
Swan was running free, straight out into a great ocean,
bound for a distant port. The actual beginning, the
umbilical cord severed—it was the culmination of five
years of preparation. Heady business, and I could hardly
believe it was happening. As if in celebration of this
auspicious debut a school of dolphins leaped playfully
around the boat. We lay on the foredeck watching those
wonderful free-spirited creatures skim and dive across
the bow. They seemed to be saying to *Swan*: "Welcome
to our world."

During those first days the combination of excitement and apprehension made sleeping difficult for me.
While we both were inexperienced, I had a greater knowledge of sailing than Molly and I was having difficulty
turning the watch completely over to her. This problem
was not lessened by the mate's tendency to overreact to
certain situations. From a deep sleep I would hear her
anxious voice: "Jimmy, I see a light!" I would leap on
deck in my underwear, expecting to be sliced in half at
any moment.

"Where is it?" I'd ask, fumbling with my glasses.

"It's over there. You can't see it all the time. Look where that big wave is right now!"

"There's big waves everywhere, for Pete's sake!"

"Come right down at an angle from that big star— it's a red light." This while drawing lines in the air with her hand.

Finally I would see a tiny speck of light from a ship, hull-down on the horizon, visible only when we were on the crest of a wave. I would determine that its course was not a threat to us and go back to bed.

Eight days out of San Francisco, near 27°N 137°W, we entered the Northeast Trades that were to blow almost continuously for the remainder of the passage. The wind pattern became predictable during the days to follow: light trades at sunrise, increasing during the day and holding steady all night.

There are few things more pleasant to a sailor than sailing day after day with 20 to 25 knots of wind on the quarter. We were making six knots in glorious sunshine under self-steering with only the large reacher poled out to leeward. With no risk of seas breaking on board we were able to keep the leeward ports and forward hatch open. A cooling breeze wafted through the boat. Fish lines were streamed out, and there was plenty of time to read and relax, or get needed work done.

This sailor's paradise was rudely interrupted one night by a furious slatting of sails. The compass read due north! The vane was hard over to one side and the cause soon became apparent. One of the stainless steel control lines leading down to the rudder servo had work-hardened and broken. It was a daylight problem. A turn of one hour each at the helm, staring at the faintly lit compass, was more than enough helm duty. At 0200 we hove to. With the boat well lighted, we set the alarm at one-hour intervals and slept until dawn.

In daylight the problem seemed less formidable. Attaching a lifting line to the vane's rudder we managed to get it on board without damaging anything. I replaced the stainless steel cable with 3/16" dacron line and we were ready to put the rudder back in place. This was the beginning of a frustrating ordeal. The boat was rolling and the wind was driving the boat at two knots. The rudder post had to be pulled up through a loose-tolerance bearing. This problem was compounded by the rolling motion of the boat.

I am not a patient man. I have always regarded interminable patience not as a virtue, but as a convenient excuse for not biting the bullet and resolving the problem at hand. The motion of the boat was thwarting my every effort, and this quickly exhausted my minuscule reserve of patience. So I resorted to swearing like a trooper at the vane. Unfortunately, the mate isn't very long on patience either. She quickly tired of my approach to the problem and let me know about it in no uncertain terms. She also knows how to soothe the savage beast and brought me a cup of coffee. We let the accursed rudder drag behind the boat and ate breakfast, during which I surreptitiously mouthed a few choice words in the vane's direction.

Suddenly the solution dawned on me. We were powerless to stop the roll but we could easily stop the forward motion. With renewed spirit we attacked the problem. We started the engine and backed the boat toward the wind until the forward motion stopped. The rolling was now the only obstacle. I held a steady pull on the lines, and when the boat rolled there was an instant when the shaft and bearing were in alignment. On about the third attempt the shaft entered the bearing and I pulled it into position. Thirty minutes later we were back on course with the vane steering.

In the early days of the voyage the self-steering vane

was something of a prima donna, demanding adjustments and refinements. I never tolerated this very well. When we would veer off course and it was the vane's fault I would storm back to the stern and growl, "What the hell is going on, Vane?" I always called him Vane. No cute names that other vanes get, as if they were part of the family. He was purchased with hard cash, and was a fabrication of metal, pure and simple. I would grasp his stainless steel neck and give it a sharp twist and the boat would correct.

As time went by the mechanical kinks were worked out and Vane gradually became more of a trusted crewmember than the mutinous scoundrel he first appeared to be. Despite my earlier resolutions to the contrary, Vane took on his own personality, partly because his job was normally performed by a human. This tended to elevate him above, say, the bilge pump. We found ourselves humanizing him more and more. There were times, especially on a long passage, that the galley just wasn't big enough for both the mate and the skipper. I would rip the lid off a beer can and go back to the stern and sit next to Vane. He would listen to me in his tacit way—I grew quite fond of him.

With the constant fair wind, life on board *Swan* had fallen into a comfortable routine. Molly prepared two meals each day, eaten in late morning and early evening. The freezer allowed us a varied diet similar to living on land. Cabbage kept better than lettuce, so it was tossed salad the first week, coleslaw the second week, alfalfa sprouts the third. The skipper was also the sprout grower. It required three days to produce a quart of sprouts. Farming began when the mate announced red alert on the cabbage supply.

The freezer also supplied us with ice—a great luxury at sea on boats the size of *Swan*. One hour of running the engine each day was sufficient to recharge the batteries and pull down the refrigeration for a 24-hour hold-over period. Two freshwater tanks held a total of 128 gallons, which allowed careful but not rationed consumption. An electric pump supplied unlimited salt water to the galley for washing dishes, which were then rinsed in fresh. Bathing was usually a cockpit affair. A dark-colored plastic jerry can filled with salt water and placed in a sunny corner of the cockpit would heat to a pleasant temperature for bathing, and we would follow with a freshwater rinse. (Joy soap lathers well in salt water.)

The skipper's efforts at farming the sea was another story altogether. All of our fishing gear was just too light. Large fish would snap the leader like thread. I kept fashioning more bizarre arrangements in a futile effort to land one. As a result of one particularly hostile raid on my shaky equipment, everything was wiped out but the hand line. I gave up.

Some months later, at Molokai, an old Hawaiian fellow took one look at the contents of my tackle box, grunted, and jerked his thumb in the direction of the rubbish bin. He then proceeded to instruct me in the art of catching deep-water fish. He showed me the lures and how to set up proper gear. It would be different on the next passage. The playing field was level now.

The halfway point was well behind us. We entered a period of excellent daily runs that were achieved with minimal effort, including one run of 164 miles with only the poled-out reacher driving the boat. We were now hopelessly spoiled, far too early in the game. Future passages would be judged and found wanting when measured against that exhilarating run for the islands. A 21-day downhill sleighride through the heart of the Indian Ocean two years later would finally set a new standard, but a lot of rocky road lay sandwiched in between.

During this passage, one storybook full-moon night stands out sharply in my memory. It was a night of perfect harmony between boat, wind, and sea—a joy to experience.

At 0200 Molly wakes me, her four-hour watch completed. I listen drowsily to the sound of water on the hull; the pleasant sounds of a yacht running before the wind. I put on jeans and a sweatshirt against the light windchill in the tropical night. The mate hands me a cup of coffee. She tells me her estimate of the course and speed made good, reminds me of the course, and minutes later is ensconced in the lee bunk. My eyes are growing accustomed to the moonlit night. The only other cockpit illumination is a small red reading light and the glow of the compass light.

A perfect Force 5 steady wind drives the boat at six knots with only the reacher set. The moon is about 20 degrees above the horizon, almost directly ahead on our course, sending a swath of lunar reflection to light the way. A small adjustment to the vane and we are sailing down the lighted pathway. I am intrigued by this unusual circumstance and consider waking Molly to see it, but don't. A 360-degree scan of the horizon assures me that *Swan* alone occupies our 30-square-mile world of sea and sky. I open my book, *Airborne*, by W. F. Buckley, and read half a chapter. A tapping sound of line against metal needs to be stopped. I know without looking that it's the pole-lift halyard. My harness tether catches on a jam cleat as I start forward; it almost always does. It irritates me and I give it a hard jerk which merely jams it harder. On the mildly heaving foredeck I adjust the shock cord on the halyard and stop the noise. The moon's azimuth has changed and *Swan* is no longer sailing down the Yellow Brick Road. Crouching in the bow, facing aft, I listen to the swishing sound of the bow cutting through the water. I look aloft as the masthead light scribes small arcs against the sky. The set of the sails is good.

I return to the cockpit, checking for line chafe as I go. A glance at the compass—close enough! I read another chapter of *Airborne*. The sun will be returning soon, and I must work up the star sights. Star sights morning and evening now. We are nearing the islands and all of those official-looking positions on the chart have been placed there by a fledgling navigator. They will gain authenticity only when the big island of Hawaii is raised on target. A faint glow lights the eastern sky. I wake the mate to help with the stars.

On the evening of the seventeenth day of the passage a four-star fix placed us 50 miles east of Hilo. At 2100 we hove to. This began an anxious night of short naps and watches, straining our eyes for any sign of land. The wind and current were setting us toward land, which wasn't doing my nerves any good even though the chart clearly showed the coast to be well-lighted.

Lack of self-confidence was now rampant. A jumble of negative thoughts raced through my mind. I worked the star sights again and plotted them, checking the date and time, looking for a gross blunder. There wasn't any. The sights had been excellent. If the island wasn't dead west about 35 miles away I would never trust any of my fixes again. How could I find a tiny speck of an atoll in the vast Pacific Ocean if I couldn't find Hawaii? The hell with it! If it isn't smack in front of us in the morning we'll turn around, go back, and sell the boat before we kill ourselves! Even I can find North America!

An anxious call from the mate saved me from a mental meltdown. "Jimmy, I see something!" In a flash I was on deck. The binoculars hanging around my neck took a hard bash against the companionway in the process.

"I saw something over there," she said, pointing off into the blackness.

"What do you mean? What was it?"

"It was a flash of light. I only saw it once."

"If you saw a light, say *light*. *Something* sounds like a big *rock* or something!"

Taking a rough bearing from the steering compass I looked through the glasses in the direction where the most powerful navigation light would be if our position were correct. Suddenly I saw it! I jumped on the dinghy on the cabintop and steadied myself against the boom. There it was again! I counted to myself, a thousand one, a thousand two...a thousand six, flash! Three times I checked it. There was no doubt. It was the 19-mile, 6-second light on Cape Kumukahi, the easternmost point on the island, 20 miles southeast of Hilo Bay. That distant flash was the confirmation of all those marks on the chart and the skill of the navigator who had put them there. A feeling of pride filled me, sweeping away the nagging doubts. I turned to the mate and announced in a voice now brimming over with confidence, "It's the Cape Kumukahi light." I knew she was glad she married me.

THE 56-FOOT ferro-cement ketch, *Starshine*, out of San Francisco, moved slowly toward the vacant berth next to us in Radio Bay, the small yacht harbor at Hilo where we tied stern to the quay, Tahiti style. Her anchor was let go and when the line was snubbed she swung slowly around and was warped into the berth, dwarfing *Swan*. We soon met her skipper Doug Balcomb, his wife Linda, and ten-year-old daughter, Heather. We were to become good friends during the following months of cruising the Hawaiian Islands.

The Hilo stop was far different from the one at San Francisco. The trip to the laundromat was merely a chore, not an ordeal. The boat required very little attention after the 18-day passage, which further attested to *Swan*'s seaworthiness. A trip to the friendly Safeway store and we were ready for the 120-mile run to Lahaina, Maui. With a wave to the crew of *Starshine* we motored out through the breakwaters.

It was midnight when we entered the Alenuihaha Channel, a 35-mile stretch of notoriously rough water between the islands of Hawaii and Maui. Rain squalls propelled by 40-knot winds came one after another, reducing visibility to nearly zero as *Swan* raced across the channel flying the jib and trysail. At dawn we sailed into the lee of Maui, where there wasn't a breath of wind to be found. This we would find to be typical of sailing conditions in Hawaiian waters: all or nothing.

Lahaina, Maui was a favorite port of call in the 1880s for the men of the wind-driven whaling ships, Hawaii's early tourist trade. We anchored for a week in the roadstead off Lahaina. This was our first and, from a comfort viewpoint, worst anchorage we were ever to experience. A swell runs constantly and the boats respond by rolling. Most nights at sea were more restful than nights anchored at Lahaina Roads.

The old watering holes along the waterfront, like the Pioneer Inn with its wooden sidewalks, maintain a flavor of a bygone era. However, the prices easily kept pace with the times. This, coupled with the miserable anchorage, was more than enough reason to leave.

At Lanai, the pineapple island, we found a spot that epitomized that idyllic setting one imagines during the long years of building; the mental fuel to keep the project moving. It was a small leeward inlet called Hulopoe Bay or locally known as White Manele. The bay is superb—crystal clear water, excellent sand bottom for anchoring, well-developed coral formations, white sand beach, and the absence of any appreciable swell. On most mornings a group of dolphins would swim lazily through the bay on their feeding rounds and paid little attention to us as we snorkeled the reefs among them. In the late afternoon we gathered keawe wood on nearby slopes for barbecues on the beach. Solar-heated freshwater showers provided the final touch of perfection. We returned to White Manele several times during our stay in Hawaii, our favorite spot by far of the places we visited in this island chain.

The new year found us on the island of Molokai. We still cringe when we recall our entrance into the small harbor at Kaunakakai. We were motoring much too fast, without the benefit of a harbor chart. The chart would have shown us that the harbor shoals rapidly near the end of the wharf, where a large gathering of people were waiting for the inter-island ferry. A small group of Hawaiian men began waving vigorously at us. We cheerfully waved back. Now their waves became frantic, with both arms up and head shaking No! No! No! Suddenly Molly shouted, "Seven feet!" Then I saw them—rows of delicate small-mesh nets for catching bait fish.

A boat anchored to port and the wharf close to starboard prevented us from turning. Full reverse! The water churned and boiled. We could feel the eyes boring into us. At last we stopped with *Swan*'s bow just touching the outer row of nets. Mercifully, at that moment the ferry screamed into the harbor on spidery hydrofoils with jet engines whining. All eyes were diverted to it and away from the asinine performance in the center ring. We backed away from the nets and continued in reverse, lest we expose the boat's name unnecessarily, and dropped the hook in a secluded spot in the harbor.

Starshine was there; it was party time. The days were taken up with reef fishing and roaming the island. At night there were potlucks, games, guitars, ukuleles, and general intemperance. Doug taught me three new chords to play on the baritone uke, which at once doubled my chord inventory and opened new musical vistas. The mate had long since tired of my two-song repertoire, even when I gave them my special calypso beat. Even now she grimaces if she hears the strains of "You Are My Sunshine."

With six chords now at my disposal I aspired to greater musical heights. The result has been a variation of the Peter Principle, for now I play long and loudly at the threshold of my level of incompetence.

However, parties on cruising yachts are not generally known for things discriminating. I was once introduced by an Aussie at a bash on the Coral Coast of Australia as an American musician. This stretched the term's definition to the breaking point, and he had previously heard me play! But parties on *Swan* Down Under were always successful, despite any musical talent deficiencies, because I knew the words to "Waltzing Mathilda" and South Australian wine flowed freely. Parenthetically, a mixture of bleach and water removes red wine stains from fiberglass instantly.

Heather and I became good friends. I was the embodiment of life in her beloved hand-puppet, Oliver. Heather was aware that I was older than she—I believe she thought I was at least 12. We would go for sails around the harbor together in our dinghy, *Cygnet*. Before picking her up on one of these outings I sailed the dinghy into the shallow water covering the reef with the centerboard raised and found there were several inches of water to spare under the boat. Later, as we skimmed along I made several reckless passes near the reef to the great alarm of my young mate.

"Jim, watch out! There's the reef!" Which I then loudly disclaimed as a needless concern.

Without her being aware I raised the centerboard as we zipped downwind dead at the reef. Again she shouted, "Watch out for the reef!"

"Don't be silly Heather, there's plenty of water covering the ree—" BAM! We piled headlong into the front of the dinghy. It had not occurred to me that while the range is small there is still a tide in Hawaii—and it was outward bound.

Cygnet suffered a gash in her stem and I suffered the righteous censuring of Heather as I rowed us back to *Starshine*. I can hear her now: "I *told* you there was a reef!"

With the new year came a reminder of things as they had been for so many years. Our W-2 forms and income-tax papers arrived, forwarded by our good friends Chuck and Florence Schmiel, who were kind enough to send our mail ahead throughout the voyage. My final

paycheck also arrived with "General Motors Corporation" printed boldly across it. No more Big Brother, no
more regular income.

Gooseneck barnacles were beginning to grow on
Swan's bottom as the existing antifouling paint wasn't
suitable for the tropics. We hauled the boat out of the
water on a marine railway at Ala Wai Marine in Honolulu,
better known as Pete's, applied two coats of tropical
paint on the undersides, and took advantage of the
yard's proximity to a shopping center to provision the
boat.

In April 1978 we sailed for Christmas Island in the
Line Islands, two degrees north of the equator, 1160
miles due south of Honolulu. *Starshine* had sailed for
the Marquesas one month earlier. Our plan was to meet
at Opua, Bay of Islands, New Zealand, on November 1.

5

THE LOOM of Honolulu's lights was still visible 50 miles away as *Swan* pushed south on a beam reach into the black Pacific night. Molly was asleep and I was on watch. Seven months had passed since we left Portland and we had not yet been on foreign soil. Had we learned anything by our lengthy sojourn in Hawaii? Daydreaming at the helm on the windward side of Maui I nearly let the boat set down on the rocks of that thundering lee shore. It scared the hell out of me! At Pokai Bay on Oahu our anchor wedged in coral, resulting in a bent shank. We dove to check the set of the anchor whenever possible after that. Hawaii introduced us to the menace of the reef, although those reefs paled in comparison to the coral labyrinths of the South Pacific and Australia's Great Barrier Reef. Taken together, the coastal work, the passage of Hawaii, and the inter-island sailing experience had molded us into more cautious, competent sailors.

Three days out and the heavens were gradually changing. The Southern Cross was prominent and Polaris was low on the northern horizon. Day and night we sailed south with the winds fair from the east. High humidity was an oppressive problem, made worse while cooking. It suddenly occurred to me that we were not in a yacht race, so why not stop the boat during the dinner period, open the ports, and be comfortable. We did, every night of that passage.

It became an evening ritual. Bring the bow through the wind and back the jib. Ease out the main and put the helm down. Open the ports and let the breeze blow through the boat. Pour a glass of burgundy and watch the sunset in the middle of the ocean. The lemmings were learning.

Snap! The spring clamp securing the loop of shock absorbing tubing on one of the trolling lines let go. A fish on! Bursting out of the water it flashed iridescent green. Its blunt head and long dorsal fin was unmistakable— our long-sought dorado. These spirited creatures live near the surface, feeding primarily on flying fish, and are among the fastest of the fishes. Hand over hand I pulled in the trolling line. Again the fish leaped completely out of the water, flashing waves of purple down its sides. Steadily the line came in until the fish was alongside while *Swan* plowed through the seas at six knots. Molly stood ready with the gaff, and after several attempts the fish was brought on board. I dispatched it with the stunner, the most distasteful part of fishing.

We were photographing our fine catch when the "dead" fish recovered. It nearly leaped out of the cockpit. Blood flew everywhere, congealing on contact in the blazing sun. Finally the valiant creature was subdued. The cockpit looked like a slaughterhouse. From that day on we killed all of the fish we caught with a .22-caliber rifle before bringing them aboard. This was more humane all around.

On the twelfth day of the passage I spent a great deal of time poring over the charts, consulting a Ouija board, and stroking a rabbit's foot. Christmas Island is a low piece of real estate and can easily be passed unseen from as little as eight to ten miles away. The euphoria of finding Hilo spot-on had given way to lingering doubts about my ability to find a small island, a tiny speck in the ocean.

The morning star-sights fixed our position 30 miles north of the island. My reckoning, which was at logger-heads with the Ouija board, indicated that the island would be visible at 1000. It was 0900 and the horizon was clean as a hound's tooth.

Swan was poking along in what passes for wind in the belt of equatorial calms. I had resolved to limit my horizon searches to once every 20 minutes. Then, while taking a bucket bath, I noticed a thickening of the horizon. I discounted it as a visual distortion from the combined effects of Joy dish detergent and salt water in nearsighted eyes. But a look through binoculars from atop the dinghy revealed a sight I shall never forget: the tops of palm trees standing in a line, like a row of green umbrellas, on the crisp blue horizon against a cloudless sky.

"Land ho!" I called out to the startled mate as I swaggered down the companionway.

"Christmas Island was a bummer," I wrote in the log after a stop of just a few hours. The bay was shoaled-in, which prevented us from entering the protected area. A fairly large swell was running in the roadstead outside the lagoon where we were anchored, so Molly stayed on board while I went ashore in the dinghy. The beaches inside the lagoon were littered with rusted remains of military equipment abandoned after the British and Americans suspended atomic tests on the island. What I saw didn't excite me very much, and in view of what promised to be an uncomfortable anchorage we decided to press on south.

An inventory of stores showed: fuel, 2/3 full; water, 3/4 full; freezer meats barely touched. Pago Pago, American Samoa, was 1256 miles to the southwest. We set a course to intersect the equator at 161°W, leaving tiny Jarvis Island to port.

On April 25, we crossed the equator. We had lived over 40 years on this planet, all of it in the northern hemisphere. Rational thought, usually undertaken while at anchor in some safe haven, makes light of superstitions of the sea—"beyond here be dragons" and that sort of thing. But when one finds himself in the middle of the vast Pacific Ocean (a misnomer if there ever was one) he does not fly in the face of tradition. This was King Neptune's domain and we'd better damn well not forget it! I reminded the mate that we were only three miles from land, but unfortunately it was straight down! So, steeped in this humble time-honored sailor's state of mind, we pledged undying fealty to King Neptune, and celebrated our transition from polliwogs to shellbacks with a couple of belts of brandy. Shellback Vane, true to his basic nature, steered us off toward the east, following some capricious cat's-paw puff.

We were ghosting south at one knot on a dying breeze. The jib was poled out flat, tight as a banjo string to stop the endless slatting of the sail. It had become our standard sail arrangement in the doldrums—a large fixed panel of resistance to airflow that moved *Swan* through the water on a zigzag path in response to Vane's sluggish commands. Sailing efficiency was the last consideration. Preventing chafing of our nerves and the sail was the top priority.

Then the wind died altogether. Log entry, April 27, 1978: "Noon position 2°28'S 162°17'W. Dead in the water. Reading *The Defense Never Rests*, by F. Lee Bailey. Calms! Calms! Calms!"

The doldrums! Not a breath of wind. The sea was glass. The afternoon sun sent a brain-piercing dagger of reflected light across the surface of the water. Incredibly, the bright orange lure on one of the fish lines was visible 100 feet straight down below the surface. A line from the "The Rime of the Ancient Mariner" came to mind:

"Alone on a wide wide sea, so lonely 'twas that God himself scarce seemed there to be." Samoa seemed a long way off.

We rigged a cockpit awning and tried not to fight the problem. Motoring wasn't even considered, but Mexican food was. With the aid of a couple of buckets of 84-degree seawater we had defrosted the freezer and in the process found steaks at the bottom that had been put there seven months earlier in Portland. Molly used them to prepare an elaborate Mexican dinner for which I harvested a fresh crop of alfalfa sprouts and rationed out some tortillas from our woefully inadequate supply; a provisioning oversight that we would regret. I arranged cushions in the cockpit and mixed gin and tonics with a slice of slightly shriveled lime. As the blazing sun sank beneath the horizon we dined in a strange peaceful solitude on this great placid pond as if we were on our own private luxury liner.

"For all we know we may be the last people on earth," I said to the mate who was at that moment reaching for the last corn tortilla. "The whole world could have nuked themselves into the promised land and we'd never know it." I poured myself another gin and watched the mate eat what was surely the last taco within a 1000-mile radius. "We could probably live out here forever. Plenty of fish, rainwater, a ton of sprouts. Lord knows we wouldn't have to worry about radioactive clouds blowing into this place!"

An uncalled-for barb from the mate about "dragging out your uke every night" put a damper on the evening so we turned on the masthead light and went to bed.

Dawn came with a cloudless sky, promising another scorcher. We motored for an hour to charge the systems, create a breeze, and break the monotony. Normally our wake at sea disappeared with the first wave, but in these conditions it was visible for several hundred yards behind us. I was intrigued by the long period of time it took for the boat to come to a complete stop. The fish lines slowly descended until they hung straight down. I decided to take them in. As I was doing this I noticed a school of small, curious dorado swimming around the lures. Near the surface I began jigging one of the lines. This created a cautious excitement among the school. One fish, bolder than the rest, bumped the lure just as I gave it a jerk and the hook snagged it. It swam around wildly while the others looked on anxiously. Dorado are intelligent, as fish go, and the school seemed to exhibit a concern for the plight of their comrade. I was on the verge of giving in to this display of brotherly love and releasing it when I remembered how delicious these fish can be. So I reconsidered and we poached it for dinner.

In the evening the sea began to stir. Catspaws ruffled the mirror surface of the water. *Swan* began to move silently forward, slowly gaining way. It soon became apparent that it wasn't a fluke; the wind had really returned. We brought in the doldrum rig and hanked on the large reacher. Within an hour we were making six knots, on course for Pago Pago, 17 days and 1650 miles out of Honolulu.

By evening, large seas had developed as an unwelcome by-product of the wind. We were carrying too much sail and *Swan* was taking flying leaps off the crests of the waves and occasionally burying her bow, which greatly alarmed me. The mate temporarily relieved Vane of command, steering us off the wind, and I took down the reacher in mainsail's wind shadow. In a careless moment while hanking on the jib I let the halyard shackle slip from my grasp. It snapped skyward, flying in wild flailing arcs with every roll of the boat. I flattened myself against the deck as far forward as I could get. After several passes the lethal whip wrapped itself around the spreaders. I was furious with myself and dreaded what was coming next—a trip aloft in a seaway with the ever-present threat of the wire halyard freeing itself before I could get control of it. We took in the main and set the vane to steer dead downwind under bare poles, the calmest conditions that we could create.

A horror story I had once heard, whether true or not, served a valuable purpose in that I took safety precautions I might otherwise not have taken. Supposedly, a couple sailing alone had problems that required someone to go aloft. Near spreader height the man lost his hold as the boat rolled and was beaten to death against the spar.

With this grim little tale foremost in my mind, I attached the main halyard to the bosun's chair and snapped a carabiner hook to my personal safety harness and to a short length of stout line passed around the mast in a loop. Dressed in jeans, a sweater, and deck shoes to prevent abrasion, I gave Molly the nod. As she took a strain on the winch I helped raise myself with my legs wrapped around the mast while holding onto the forward lower shroud. As the boat rolled we held steady, and when it paused momentarily a foot or so would be gained. At spreader height the G-force at the end of a roll convinced me that the horror story could very well be true. After an exhausting bout with the fouled halyard I finally snapped it to the chair and secured the wire under my arm to prevent it from hitting me in the face. The descent was made extremely difficult by the demonic whipping of the halyard, which seemed intent on cutting my arm off. When I reached the deck I could barely stand as my legs were weak and trembling from the tremendous exertion of that wild ride aloft. A halyard never got away from either of us again.

Some months later, after a few bottles of Fiji Bitter on the veranda of the Royal Suva Yacht Club, I related this sea story to some of the boys. One of them remarked that I should have taken a line up the mast with the end secured on deck, and tied off the loose halyard during the descent. It was 20-20 hindsight, but he was right.

Our route to Pago Pago via Christmas Island made good use of the Southeast Trades, and the passage was a pleasant reach instead of the beat it would have been had we sailed the direct route from Honolulu.

On the evening of the 26th day of the passage we hove to 40 miles to windward of Tutuila Island. As we sailed into Pago Pago Harbor the following morning we were greeted by the overpowering stench of the fish-processing plants.

The harbor is deep with a bottom that falls away from the shore like a side of a mountain. An impatient customs official on the shore motioned for us to drop our anchor right where we were—in 65 feet of water! A thirty-five pound anchor and all-chain rode in such deep water, at a minimum of 4:1 scope, is a whole lot of iron, and it all had to come back up! Operating a manual anchor windlass is always a chore, and is pure mule labor at those depths. But we did it. That customs man would die of old age waiting before we would do it again.

Pago Pago is a dirty, littered, hot, humid place that shows most of the typical signs of an island culture unable to cope with the problems created by the complexities of modern society being thrust upon it too quickly. A drinking nut discarded in the bush is not unsightly and returns to the soil in time. Not so with the aluminum cans, broken beer bottles, and general litter that is strewn along the shore of that polluted harbor.

Everywhere in Pago Pago one sees the ubiquitous, gaudily painted, usually run-down bus. These are privately owned and operate without set schedules. The average fare was about 25 cents when we were there, and they are an experience to ride. We boarded one without knowing its destination. The bus rumbled past the large fish-packing plant, from which emanated the obnoxious odor that permeates the bay. A few miles from Pago Pago, at the small village of Aua, we clambered over a spare tire that was lying in the aisle of the bus and ducked through the small doorway onto the hot, dusty street in front of the settlement.

The natives of the village live in thatched or corrugated metal-roofed, open-sided houses called *fales* (pronounced follis). Some of them are built traditionally, using fibrous grass and saplings. Others are constructed with modern materials in patchy uncoordinated schemes.

We saw a wide-grinning, ample-paunched, Samoan man standing in the doorway of his little store. He was wearing the traditional wraparound cloth called a *lavalava* in place of pants. He was covered with tattoos from just above his knees to his waist, and he explained to us that tattoos told a man's history, his personal traits, and notable events of his life. Courage was one of the virtues depicted, and indeed, it would take courage to have the tattoos applied, as it is done with a sharp fishtooth to very sensitive areas of the body.

The shelves of the store were meagerly stocked, with the exception of canned tunafish from the nearby packing plant and locally produced coconut oil soap. We purchased large, inexpensive bars of this soap, which we found to be an excellent shampoo in either fresh or salt water.

After a few days of Pago Pago we decided to leave. We cleared customs and immigration and moved to the fuel dock.

Taking on fuel next to us was an American oceangoing tug. It fueled for nine hours at the rate of 10,000 gallons per hour. In contrast, we required only twenty gallons after 2400 miles at sea. The chief engineer passed us a hose to top off our water tanks from their supply.

The tug's water had been taken on in Washington State, and was preferable to Pago Pago's water, which was of questionable purity. The captain invited us on board for dinner, which evolved into a party. The crew was a compatible group, and our last evening in Pago Pago a pleasant one.

The sun had been down for two hours when two seamen from the tug cast off our lines. We picked up the lighted range and motored out of the harbor into long smooth swells on a windless night.

It's 80 miles to Apia, Western Samoa—about 16 hours by sail, which meant an overnight run to arrive at midday. There is a light on the eastern tip of Upolu Island, with a nominal range of 20 miles. We set a course that would clear the island by a reasonable margin. Shortly after noon we entered the port of Apia. Overshadowing everything in the harbor was a visiting West German warship; German sailors were everywhere.

Apia is larger and cleaner than Pago Pago, and less humid. A bustling open-air market sells locally grown produce at very reasonable prices. In contrast, imported goods are expensive.

We were anxious to visit Aggie Grey's Hotel, a fixture of South Pacific lore going back decades. The evening we spent there was delightful. After an excellent dinner we met Aggie, who was then 84. The meeting was rather formal, on the order of an audience with a queen, but she soon warmed to our questions about earlier voyagers who had called there and reminisced about them. It was the highlight of our visit to Samoa.

The German navy took over the town during their four-day visit. A big dance was held for them, and we attended. The local girls were quite taken by the sailors and were clamoring to dance with them while the young Samoan men looked on angrily from the sidelines. It had all the makings of a bad scene. As I could easily have been mistaken for one of the sailors, I envisioned myself being caught up in a melee between a bunch of Samoans and the Fatherland's finest. This was high on my list of things not to do in Apia. I edged Molly toward the nearest exit.

Suddenly the band struck up "Deutschland über Alles" in honor of the visiting Germans, who were nearly all in various stages of inebriation and didn't even stop dancing. When the anthem was over the band swung smartly into a rousing, jazzed-up version of the United States Marine Corps Hymn. The couples whirled around the floor in the stifling heat as Molly and I stood there gaping, slack-jawed, in the din and glare.

There is a particularly bad aspect of visiting Western Samoa on a yacht. The Samoan's age-old culture of borrowing appears to have evolved in a negative way among some of the younger men, who consider yachts to be prime targets. Things left on deck tend to disappear. Dinghies are especially at risk. We were warned repeatedly about the problem by older Samoans and certain Samoan officials. It put a damper on evenings ashore.

Our decision to leave the island came one afternoon when two young men swam out to the boat demanding whiskey. I refused, and they began banging the hull with the anchor chain. My first thought was to break their heads with the anchor windlass handle. Curbing this impulse, I threatened to radio the harbor police. This frightened them and they left. So did we.

Our opinion of the South Pacific was becoming increasingly negative; fortunately it would soon change.

*E*NTERING OR leaving the port of Apia requires careful piloting. The entrance is guarded by reefs on which the seas break frightfully. We stood out four miles to clear a set of fringing reefs before turning west toward Apolima Strait, which divides Upolu and Savaii Islands. A fresh breeze on the starboard quarter drove us along at six knots.

Once through the straits our course to the Vava'u Group, Tonga, immediately became difficult, as we were bashing close-hauled into head seas. At sunset the wind picked up strength and veered to the east, making our course easier, but requiring a sail reduction.

During the sail change I aggravated a sore pectoral muscle that I had strained when I slipped while boarding the dinghy in Pago Pago. The mate took charge. She wrapped my chest with an elastic rib belt and put me in the bunk where, according to her account at a later date, I was the worst patient in her 18 years of nursing experience. An obvious overstatement that I attribute to the strain of sudden command.

Vava'u is an ideal landfall from the north. There are no reefs on that side of the island, and sheer cliffs rise hundreds of feet above the crashing surf. The moon was full, which enabled us to approach the island at night with a fair degree of visibility. Molly sighted the island in the moonlight just after midnight. A round of starsights using the moonlit horizon determined the distance at 13 miles. At dawn we were in the approaches to the natural channel leading to Neiafu.

The channel winds along for seven miles among small islands and, with few exceptions, the water is fairly deep a short distance from shore. The anchorage at Neiafu is like a placid lake. The bottom is studded with coral heads and occasional sandy patches. We dropped anchor in one of these patches. The abundant coral presented a strong justification for all-chain rode.

My chest was hurting so much that Molly had to do most of the work of getting the anchor down and launching the dinghy with the main halyard. The crew of a nearby yacht was observing us. I was embarrassed by my inactivity and went to great lengths to display the rib belt.

Our first contact with the islanders was reassuring after our experiences in Apia. They smiled readily, greeting us with *Malo'lalay*.

In 1820 Christian missionaries came to Tonga, and by 1850 they had converted the islands to the Christian faith. There must have been a lot of them because, according to the Tongan government, every Christian denomination is represented there.

The missionary influence is evident in the Tongan conservative mode of dress. Bare legs are not often seen. On Sunday commercial activity halts. A legal document signed on Sunday is not recognized by the Tongan government.

At six o'clock on Sunday morning a cacophony invades the tranquil bay. Church bells ring, and are accompanied by the rhythmic beating of a hollowed-out log called a *lali*. Roosters crow, and it all sets the dogs to barking in the surrounding villages. Soon, this pleasant discord is replaced by the beautiful singing of the islanders. We attended church services every Sunday to listen to the singing, even though we could not understand their language.

Laboring in the hot sun in the Vava'u Group earned about two pa'angas per day in 1978 which equated to $2.38 in U.S. currency. One island entrepreneur who decided that his talents were worth more than that was a tall, lanky fellow named Isaiah, who lived on the nearby island of Pagaimotu. Early one morning he approached us in a little boat powered by a coughing, sputtering, battered British Seagull outboard motor. He produced a shopworn letter from his pocket, written by the skipper of an earlier visiting yacht, and extolling the quality of the "Tongan feast" that Isaiah put on at his village. The fee was two pa'angas per person.

It was a cleverly written letter, containing a dual message. The primary message was that the feast was well worth attending, written in a way that Isaiah could understand. The second message went over his head: Keep the booze away from Isaiah! From memory, it was worded something like this: "Isaiah's culinary expertise and your experience will be ameliorated immeasurably by his abstention from distilled spirits or any other intoxicating beverage that might augment this gentleman's intemperate propensities." Evidently the missionaries had let one slip through the net.

Isaiah had sold the crew of another yacht on the deal, and the mate was all for it. So I shook hands with this glib-tongued Tongan and said, "A faint heart never ate roast pig." This brought forth a grunt from Isaiah, who was eyeing a gallon jug of burgundy wine in the corner of the cockpit.

"Motor oil," I said, pointing at the jug. "Engine. Petrol. Oil."

He gave me an "I wasn't born yesterday look" and I resolved to keep the demon rum out of sight on the day of the feast.

On the morning we were to meet Isaiah we spent nearly an hour unwrapping the anchor chain from around coral heads. I spent some time wrestling with the tide book, as the chart showed shoal water between our anchorage and the site of the feast. It was a mental exercise, due to the Tongan desire to be "the place where time begins." They had jogged the International Dateline so that they would be on the same day of the week as Fiji and New Zealand, but one hour earlier. Our tide book was predicated on Apia, where it is the same time as Tonga, but not the same day. Isaiah, a self-proclaimed expert pilot, was there to guide us through the shoals. He was definitely not lacking in self-confidence. He soon tired of my calculations and pointing at the shore he said, "We go when water get up to rock." I acquiesced.

True to his word, he piloted the boats through the shoals and we entered a picturesque sheltered bay where he and his family lived.

With the exception of suckling pig, which is roasted on a spit over an open fire, Tongan foods are cooked in an underground oven called an *umu*. A fire is built in a pit and allowed to cook down to coals. Rocks are then laid on the hot coals. Next, green coconut tree fronds are laid on the rocks. The food to be cooked is wrapped in banana leaves and placed on the fronds. Sticks of wood are laid across the pit and covered with banana leaves, with a final layer of coarse sand spread over them. A slow-cooking oven is the result.

If anything, Isaiah had undersold the feast. From the *umu* came lobster, crab, and *lu pulu*—small pieces of lamb or pork immersed in a cream made from the meat of the coconut, and wrapped in large taro leaves with slices of onion. Next came whole breadfruit, taro, small pieces of breadfruit cooked in rich coconut cream, and large slices of white yams. The food was served on banana leaves and we ate with our fingers.

It was a great day. After a pleasant night in a peaceful anchorage we picked our way through the shoals and sailed back to Neiafu.

A few days later a young woman named Ilaise, whom we'd met in church, called to us from the shore. I rowed over and she told us that her uncle who lived on the island of Ovaka, 10 miles southwest of Vava'u, had died. We offered transportation for her family and relatives, and she accepted.

Early the next morning 13 people boarded *Swan* at the town wharf. The ladies were dressed in long black dresses, black hats, and carried black umbrellas. The men watched intently as I hanked on the headsail and nodded at me every time our eyes met. As Molly steered the boat through the narrows (normally a man's job in Tonga) the women stared at her as if she were from another planet. Within a few minutes of leaving the dock, in the dead calm of the channel, some of the women became seasick and were leaning over the lifelines, still holding their umbrellas. The men found this very amusing, which didn't set very well with Molly, who knew firsthand the misery of *mal de mer*. I wondered what would happen when we crossed the open water near Ovaka.

Two hours and much retching later we were in the exposed anchorage at Ovaka. The men on board were directing me toward the shore. It was apparent that they were not aware that a sailboat has a keel and were treating the situation as if they were in their flat-bottom skiffs. I stood at the bow watching for coral heads, and looked back at Molly every few seconds as she hand-signaled the depth sounder readings. I sensed by the men's disapproving looks that they were interpreting this as my asking Molly's permission to drop the anchor. Later I showed them the depth sounder, which explained the situation. They were impressed with the instrument and I regained my position of skipper in their eyes.

I emphasized to Ilaise, who had spent some time in New Zealand and spoke English fairly well, the importance of returning to Neiafu before dark, as there were no navigation lights in the channel. She assured us that they would return no later than 4:00 p.m. Molly and I stayed on board. Every hour or so a boy would row out with something different to eat. No one dies of starvation at Tongan funerals.

As the afternoon wore on the funeral party straggled back to the boat one or two at a time. At five o'clock the last person, an elderly lady, was helped aboard and we were moving in less than a minute as the engine was running and the anchor barely hooked. It was a race against the clock, as there is very little twilight in the tropics. We ran before the wind across the open water in medium seas, motorsailing at seven knots. Four women, one of whom was pregnant, resumed their previous stations at the lifelines, sans umbrellas. Once in the channel, in the lee of Nuapapu Island, the seas smoothed out and the sick ladies recovered and laughed self-consciously among themselves. One woman recovered enough to play my ukulele and sing island songs while *Swan* plowed along with the engine running flat-out and sails all standing.

Ilaise's father asked to speak to me privately. Molly took the helm and we went below. After asking me some general and a few personal questions he came to the point. He asked me if we would take Ilaise back to America with us. I was at once taken aback and touched by the sincerity of his request. He then said that I could be like a daddy to her. I managed to make him understand that we would not be returning to the United States for two years or more. I also tried to imagine Molly's reaction to me being a "daddy" to a 24-year-old

Polynesian girl. The father eventually understood that the plan wasn't feasible and the matter was dropped.

Swan ran up the channel at full speed, arriving in Neiafu at dusk, and nosed into the crowded dock. After a great deal of handshaking and waving we motored to the anchorage in the dark, where, to counteract jet lag, I mixed us two large drinks of coconut water and gin, and we collapsed on the bunks.

Our remaining days at Vava'u were spent visiting the villages and homes of people we had met, and writing magazine articles. I had sold my first article, written during our stay in Hawaii, and had instantly envisioned myself as a latter-day Jack London, sending a steady flow of written adventures from the South Pacific to an ever-growing audience of avid readers anxious to share our experiences. As time went on, I attributed my failure to vault swiftly into literary stardom at least partially to the general malaise that President Carter had claimed was spreading like wildfire across the country, and to the fact that Jack London did not have to compete with television.

The realization that our bank account seemed to be locked on the final glide path was not borne easily. So, during the first three or four hours each morning the rat-a-tat-tat of the old Smith Corona could be heard emanating from the good ship *Swan*.

Our island friends took us on a shellfish-collecting expedition on the tidal flats, where their trained eyes spotted edible delicacies that we were stumbling over to their great merriment, and ours.

The situation was reversed, though, when I brought my tools ashore to repair their broken equipment. They huddled around in awe as I threaded stripped parts and fitted them with new nuts and bolts from our supplies.

We gave them spices, canned meats, medical supplies, fishing equipment, and nylon line to tether their pigs. In turn, they gave us handmade sandals, hats, baskets, and mats woven from *pandanus*. When we were preparing to leave, these gentle people came to the boat with large baskets of yams, limes, breadfruit, and coconuts, "so we wouldn't have to buy anything at the other islands." We blinked back the tears.

Two hundred years earlier Captain Cook had aptly named Tonga the Friendly Islands.

7

THE 480-MILE passage to Suva, located on the largest island in Fiji, Viti Levu, entailed a hazardous route through the Lau Group, easternmost of the Fijian islands. The Lau archipelago extends about 240 miles in a roughly north-south direction, and its reef-lined channels are beset with tricky currents. We planned this passage to coincide with a full moon, not only for its navigational aid, but because scary things at night are less scary in the moonlight.

In the age of lasers and microwave popcorn, superstitions and myths about the moon still persist. It is the one celestial body that can serve as a guidepost to the mariner not only at night, but often during the day. One of the quickest and easiest celestial positions that can be obtained at sea is a noon latitude by the sun crossed with a line of position from the moon. No running fix; just cross them. At night the moon often illuminates the horizon sufficiently to take star-sights at the convenience of the navigator rather than during the inflexible time limits of nautical twilight. Still, I've heard many hollow arguments against the moon as the horizon illuminator for nocturnal star-sights.

I had been involved in a heated discussion of this subject one evening at a gathering of sundry seadogs in Honolulu after a sufficient quantity of beer had been consumed to lubricate any argument. It culminated in the chief skeptic and me clambering out on the breakwater, sextant in hand, for the acid test. One shot each of Sirius by the light of the moon. The LOP from my sight crossed within a half mile—a good shot. Chief Skeptic's LOP actually crossed the breakwater about 100 yards from where he took it, which was astounding, especially considering Chief Skeptic's condition at the time. He crowed about it all night. We could hardly shut him up.

Our first day out of Vava'u resulted in a nice run of 147 miles. That ended the nice runs. The wind was all over the compass at varying strengths, then settled from the northwest at Force 6. We slammed into the seas in a driving rain. Molly was queasy, so I took the watch all night. Not that I could have slept anyway, bearing down toward danger as we were.

I had selected the 34-mile-wide channel dividing Vatoa Island and Nuku Songe Reef to pass through the group. The current sets south there at that time of year, but I had no real estimate of its effect on our course. The DR position showed us to be 50 miles east of the passage. It was a cold fish and I had little faith in its accuracy. I peered over the dodger through the pelting rain and spray into the blackness. No help from our friend the moon in this weather! My mind's eye visualized huge combers crashing on a reef just ahead. We couldn't be that close yet—surely not! It was like trying to run through a hole in a fence blindfolded. I no longer had a firm grip on the situation. I went by the book and hove to. The frightening beat to windward was immediately replaced by that strange state of calm suspension which allows the brain to function without the panicky pressure of dire consequence. I went below to study the chart. Our position seemed safe—we would keep a careful watch.

At dawn the skies had cleared enough to take a round of star sights. These fixed our position 22 miles east of the passage. We soon sighted Vatoa Island and passed close enough for positive identification.

One more squeeze play was in front of us. We had to pass between two islands that had fringing reefs extending out eight to ten miles. As if on cue, the wind backed all the way around to the southwest, forcing us to tack north of the northern island. Rounding the island we saw the hulk of a wrecked freighter high, dry, and rusty on the reef. It marked the outer edge of the reef; we drew away from the island close-hauled on the starboard tack into safe water.

At 0300 I noticed a flicker of light on the horizon. Within an hour the city lights of Suva were distinguishable. A welcome landfall. In the early afternoon we were anchored near the quarantine buoy in Suva Harbor, awaiting pratique.

Fiji's population is comprised of about half native Fijians and half Indians, with a sprinkling of Europeans and other islanders. The Indians were first brought to Fiji by the English as indentured laborers to work in the sugar industry. When their contractual period of labor ended, most of the Indians stayed in Fiji, scratching out a meager living by any means available.

The two major races appear to live completely independent of each other. The Indians dominate the government jobs and run the duty-free shops. Like in so many ports around the world, the motto is "Buyer beware". Prices are incredibly inflated and business is conducted with such flagrant misrepresentation that it would have made Phineas T. Barnum blanch.

The filmy saris of the Indian women contrast sharply with the colorfully printed clothing worn by the Fijian women. The aroma of curry from the Indian restaurants permeates the marketplace where vegetables, eggs, fish, squawking live chickens, island handicraft, and other goods are hawked by both races in a highly competitive manner. Indian sidewalk merchants point at a gaudy array of costume jewelry, imploring the passerby to "have a look, have a look." We soon caught on to the way of it.

With our canvas carrying-bag stuffed with inexpensive produce we would make our way to the buses, through the crowds of commuters, past the Indian peanut-vendors. Fending off the platoons of newsboys chanting in high-pitched voices "Fiji Sun—Fiji Times," we would board the bus and pay the nine-cent fare for the lurching, reckless ride to the yacht club.

It's easy to homestead in a port like Suva, but we wanted to explore the outer islands. Molly put the necessary provisions on board and I attended to the needs of *Swan*. We purchased a bundle of *yagona* root for preparing kava, and parceled it into smaller packets to be used as gifts to the village chiefs.

Kava is Fiji's national drink. It's made from the mildly narcotic *yagona* and is drunk as a symbol of welcome and friendship. It causes a numbing effect on the tongue and lips when drunk in fairly large quantities. It has a rather muddy taste.

We were ready for our excursion when the weather took a turn for the worse. It was winter in Fiji, an unpredictable season. High-winds were forecast, and they soon hit the island, bringing rain and heavy seas. The seas crashed on the barrier reef with tremendous force. Strong winds swept across the harbor, causing several boats to drag their anchors. It was not the time to leave Suva.

It was snug lying in the bunk reading a book at night with the wind singing through the rigging. We felt comfortable and safe. Day after day the wind and rains came. There were card games and movies at the Royal Suva Yacht Club, and endless conversations on the veranda to while away the time.

Every morning we would look seaward for an indication of change. The seemingly endless black clouds scudded swiftly overhead with an occasional patch of blue. High winds continued and the seas kept building with the unlimited fetch to the southeast. Boats with crews clad in foul weather gear sailed into the harbor, but none were leaving; the anchorage was becoming crowded. Talking about the weather was becoming an obsession.

One morning just before dawn we were awakened by the gentle rolling motion of the boat. The wind had died and a calm had descended on the bay. The boats at anchor were no longer rigidly faced off to the southeast; they had assumed random positions and their masts were swaying in the gentle swell. The sky was clear; the high-wind warnings were cancelled. Sunrise was accompanied by the sound of anchor chains being taken in.

There are many places to visit in Fijian waters and our plans were flexible. A gentle westerly was getting up, so we set a course for Kandavu Island in the Great Astrolabe Reef, 40 miles due south. A month of diving and exploring the islands would be perfect before our departure for New Zealand. After all, Molly had said she thought we needed a short vacation.

A heavy swell generated by many days of high winds slowed our progress, but it was pleasant to feel the deck rise and fall to the seas once again under a cloudless sky.

In the late afternoon we approached Usborn Pass, a narrow opening at the northern end of the reef. To the southeast mighty combers crashed with a continuous roar on the barrier reef, sending white water flying in the air. Nervously I stood on the bow and conned the boat through the rocks and coral heads, using a prearranged set of hand signals for the mate to steer by.

The lagoon inside the Great Astrolabe Reef measures approximately 120 square miles, with several islands and islets scattered about. One larger island, Ono, occupies the southern part. Sailing conditions are nearly perfect inside the lagoon—the tradewinds sweep across it without the accompanying heavy seas, thanks to the reef. However, one must keep a good accounting of the way of the ship as there are sporadic patches of rock and coral to contend with.

The sun was low in the sky when we dropped our anchor in the lee of Mara Island—small, uninhabited, skirted by a shimmering white sand beach. Coconut-laden palms were gently swaying in the breeze. We gazed for a time at the setting, straight out *Tales of the South Pacific*. We wasted no time getting ashore.

There is something eerie about an uninhabited island. Perhaps it's that one doesn't really believe it. The natives from nearby islands make periodic visits to Mara Island to harvest coconuts. They remove the copra, and the husks in the bush are the only evidence of human life there. The beach was covered with shells, and Molly added several to her collection. We discovered a rock formation that could serve as a barbecue pit, and later that evening we baked a fish we had caught en route, under a full moon.

The true marvel of the island is that it is not an exception. In the Fijian group there are dozens of islands offering substantially the same untouched beauty. We buried or carried away our refuse, leaving the islands exactly as we had found them.

Jim and Lucille Parker on *Giselle*, a 44-foot sloop from Bainbridge, Washington, were also sailing in the lagoon. They had met a native diver named Pana on the island of Ndruvuni, and had arranged a diving expedition to the barrier reef. They invited us to join them.

Molly and I have an inordinate fear of sharks, perhaps because of the profusion of killer-shark movies and television documentaries on the subject. Many times we had snorkeled on the reef in the bays and lagoons, but never in shark country!

Courage in numbers. Fourteen people, including the natives, boarded *Giselle* for the trip to the reef, with three dinghies in tow. Pana piloted the boat to a shoal area where, with some trepidation, we boarded the small boats and rowed to the reef.

Over the side we went wearing diving masks and snorkels. As the briny closed over me I thought of the documentary where Great White sharks tore through chunks of horsemeat with a violent shaking action before savagely attacking the caged photographers. I made several quick revolutions to be sure that some mindless brute hadn't zeroed in on me for its afternoon repast.

The visibility was incredibly good. A school of yellowfin tuna swam slowly by without registering any fear. Their apparent absence of fear was reassuring as I had always believed, without substantiation, that fish would sense the presence of a shark and react long before a man would. On the other hand, I had read somewhere that dodo birds are extinct because they were too dumb to fear their enemies. I never dropped my guard for an instant.

After a while I relaxed enough to enjoy the spectacular world of the reef. Sunlight refracting through the surface of the water created a shimmering accent to the many hues intrinsic to the reef. A profusion of brilliantly colored fish poked about in the coral formations, hunting and being hunted. Life hangs on a tenuous thread in this underwater world.

Eventually we all straggled back to *Giselle*. Pana had speared a moray eel and caught a large lobster. He casually remarked that a few days earlier two sharks, 10 to 12 feet long, had swum so close to him that he was forced to prod them away with his spear. Flashing a toothy smile he said, "No worry about."

Kavala Bay, at Kandavu Island, looked interesting on the chart. It was a beautiful two-hour sail with a fresh breeze on the quarter. The bay reminded us of Vava'u, with similar shoreline characteristics and dense flora extending nearly to the water's edge. We soon discovered that the similarities did not end there. The people of Soloavul, a small village on the bay, were just as friendly as the Tongans.

We anchored near the mouth of a stream close to shore. Children in dugout canoes paddled out to greet us, waving and shouting as we put the dinghy over the side. The normal chore of lugging the dinghy onto the beach was carried out by nearly a dozen children, who waded into the water and whisked the dinghy onto high ground.

A pleasant young woman, Siteri Tui, welcomed us to her village in halting English. We presented the *yagona* root to her as a gift to the village and were subsequently invited to a kava ceremony and dance that evening.

The children clustered around us as we walked through the village. I was impressed with the sanitation facilities the Fijian government had built there. Pure water is piped in from the mountains under gravity pressure wherever possible. When we returned to our dinghy we were pleasantly surprised to find that our water jugs had been filled by the children.

In the evening we went ashore with the Parkers, who were anchored nearby. Outside the meeting house, a roughly built structure, a man was pulverizing *yagona* root with a hardwood pole in a heavy wooden container. A pale yellow light shone through the door of the meeting house onto the dirt path.

Every eye was on us as we entered the crowded room. The village elders were seated on mats on the floor. Not knowing if they were seated in order of age or rank I gambled on shaking hands left to right with the greeting *ni sa bula*. Their stern facade partially crumbled as we shook hands. We sat facing them as the kava was served by a slender young woman in an ankle length dress. The elders were served first in order of age; the oldest first. The two men in our party were served next, again in order of age. The women were served last by the same guidelines. Fiji is a paradise for an elderly male chauvinist.

When the ceremony was over the music began. A guitar and ukulele were their only instruments. A rhythmical beat was provided by a group of girls who alternately clapped their hands and pounded the floor in unison.

I studied the faces of the older men. Their grandfathers could very well have been cannibals. The remoteness of the village and my runaway imagination vividly brought home the courage of the early missionaries. But that was a long time ago. I felt guilty for even conjuring up the thought as fun-loving young women curtsied and tapped their chosen dancing partners on the knee.

They nearly danced us to exhaustion and our feet were raw from the coarsely woven *pandanus* mats. We danced in their style, but I managed to slip in a little wild rock-and-roll to great peals of laughter from the young girls.

The children loved Molly. She would join in their games and often had small treats for them in her bag. On one occasion she popped enough popcorn to fill a five-gallon plastic bag. She set it on the ground and invited the throng of kids to help themselves. It was obvious that they had never seen popcorn before. They reached into the bag and daintily took one kernel each and ate it. "No, no, no, like this!" I said, as I grabbed a large handful and ate it. In a flash about 20 yelling kids pounced on the bag and scooped up the corn, stuffing it into their mouths and pockets. In a few minutes there wasn't a kernel left.

We extended an open invitation to the people of the village to come aboard *Swan* for an inspection. Several adults and nearly all of the kids did.

During this visit I noticed a furtive conversation between two boys about 12 years of age. Having raised two daughters, and with the benefit of empirical knowledge gained by having once been twelve myself, I sensed some chicanery afoot. The reason for the whispering was soon apparent: Two stainless steel rigging knives that were kept in pouches by the companionway ladder were gone. They had evidently presented an irresistible temptation to this pair of lads.

Later, on the beach, I approached one of the boys and suggested that perhaps he could assist us in getting the persons who "borrowed" the knives to return them. I told him that I intended to speak with the village chief to see if he could also help in locating the borrowed knives. The color in his face turned several shades lighter at the mention of the chief. As we walked along I could see him from the corner of my eye talking earnestly with his friend, who was also becoming a very light-complexioned Fijian as the word "chief" was uttered.

I had no intention of sullying our visit with the gracious people of this village by making an issue of the missteps of a couple of young boys. I planned to see the chief about something totally different and let the band of two assume it was about the knives. It never came to that.

One of the boys ran breathlessly up to me and explained that he had found the errant knives by an old rotten boat on the beach where the other kids must have been using them when they were lost. I had to bite my lip to keep from laughing. He was very concerned about whether I still intended to talk to the chief and was visibly relieved when I told him it would no longer be necessary.

Two thoughts about the incident crossed my mind. One, the boys must now believe, if we bought that story, that Americans must be among the most gullible people on the face of the earth, and two, there are a great number of cities in the United States that could use a few chiefs!

It was time to leave. We offered transportation to Suva for as many people as we could safely carry. The fee to ride the inter-island ferry from Kandavu to Suva was $13, inordinately expensive when one considers that a man labors two or three days for that amount on the other islands. Five men accepted the offer.

Early on the morning we were to leave, two flat-bottomed boats came alongside. One carried the five men who were leaving, plus several children who had come along for the ride. The other boat was loaded to the gunwales with bales of *yagona* root, *pandanus*, bottles of coconut oil, and various other goods bound for the Suva market. What an oversight! We hadn't even considered that marketing their goods was the primary reason they were going to Suva. It was typical of islanders not to mention the freight.

We were not in the least prepared for the cargo and it wasn't the type of things that could be lashed on deck. We dug out a tarpaulin and spread it over the cabin sole and settees. On this we stacked the bales, bundles, and bags. It required a feat of gymnastics to get from the cockpit to the head.

At last everyone was on board and I was dripping with sweat. A great deal of waving and shouting takes place when a boat leaves a Fijian village, and our departure was no exception as we eased out of the bay toward the pass. Soon we were clear of the reef, with a fresh southeasterly pushing our heavily laden boat towards

Suva. The shadows of the clefts in the mountains on Kandavu gradually faded into a blue-gray haze.

I handed a pair of binoculars to one of the men and pointed toward Kandavu. Invariably the islanders would look through the wrong ends. It amused me to watch their puzzled expressions over the possible reasons why anyone would want to make something appear farther away and smaller than it actually is. They passed the glasses to one another, each taking their turn looking through them and muttering amongst themselves. Eventually I turned the glasses around and they laughed loudly when they realized I had been putting them on.

A school of yellowfin hit our lures and we landed two of them, which provided some excitement. The Fijians were intensely interested in our fishing equipment and the manner in which we used it. I added to the mystique by explaining that the lures were from Hawaii, which set off a big discussion among the men.

The awesome power of the surf crashing on the barrier reef guarding Suva Harbor is difficult to adequately describe. The bones of many ships lie scattered along that treacherous coast. That misjudged light, an ill-timed storm—different tales with the same ending. We motorsailed through the channel with sails all standing.

Docking near the central market taxed every area of our knowledge of maneuvering a boat in a confined place. After a Fijian version of a Chinese fire drill, our passengers and their cargo, including the two fish that we gave them, were deposited on shore. We managed to get away from the dock with nothing more than a small scratch on the hull to remind us to always pay heed to surge in harbors.

8

OUR STAY in Fiji had stretched into three months. The Tasman Sea was waiting. We had heard many stories about this treacherous body of water—depressions, anti-cyclones, late winter gales, early tropical cyclones, and perhaps a Tasmanian devil here and there. The 75-foot schooner *Constellation* had returned to Fiji after losing a four-day bout with a Tasman special, and this didn't do anything positive to our state of mind.

Departure preparations were put on the back burner with the arrival of the *U.S.S. Horne*, a cruiser, and the destroyer *U.S.S. Robison*. We were given a special tour of the *Horne* and treated to an excellent seafood dinner. In the natural order of things, several men from the *Horne* joined us for a Sunday-night barbecue and beer blast at the yacht club. It had been a long time since we'd heard such a barrage of American slang. The next day one of the club members, an older, graying gentleman who fairly exuded 19th Century British colonialism asked me in his dry way, "I say, what is that language you Yanks speak?" Later, when we were leaving for New Zealand, his parting shot as we shook hands was, "You know, they speak English there."

Our cruising itinerary was evolving. Three of my articles had been published in sailing magazines, which encouraged me in at least some of my writing goals. Captain Cook's voyage of exploration through Australia's Great Barrier Reef and Captain Bligh's open-boat voyage to Timor after the *Bounty* mutiny had captured our interest. We wanted to trace their routes through the reef and write about it along the way. The catch was getting back out of the reef without beating ourselves senseless against the Southeast Trades. The answer was Greeley-esque: Go West! We were now thinking in terms of circumnavigation.

This decision revealed a severe shortage in our chart inventory, and precipitated a flurry of horse-trading of charts with other yachts. The quartermaster on the *Horne* asked me if we were short any charts for our westward voyage. I answered, "Everything west of Port Moresby." He said that he was about to discard a large stack of outdated charts of the Indian and Atlantic Ocean areas. Would I like to look through them first? I nearly knocked him down getting up the gangway. This windfall closed a large part of the chart gap.

That lucky break was followed by a similar one a few months later in Sydney. We were still in need of most of the Caribbean charts and were resigned to purchasing the excellent but expensive British Admiralty publications. I telephoned a large chart house to check on their availability, and the proprietor said that he had a bundle of more than a hundred American charts, many of which covered our area of interest. They had been ordered for a ship that sailed without paying for them; he was stuck with them, and he would sell them for a dollar each if I took them all. Before I could answer, he said he was sick and tired of stumbling over them, and on second thought, if I would pick the charts up that afternoon he would give them to me free of charge!

We made it across town by bus in less than an hour. As we were leaving with this treasure trove we shook hands and he thanked me twice for "taking the bloody things off my hands." I couldn't recall another time that

I had so thoroughly enjoyed doing such a magnanimous favor for someone.

The Southeast Trades were in full swing as we sailed out of Suva Harbor into a heavy ground swell. Molly was at the helm in her Brer Bear hat, a sloppy straw affair she wore as a first line of defense against the tropical sun. At 0900 we cleared the channel. At 0905 we took a green sea over the bow. Was this a harbinger of things to come? I harbor not a scintilla of superstition about anything whatsoever; still, I had a sense of foreboding about this passage. The tasks at hand and the beautiful sunny day managed to dispel my gloomy thoughts.

The Bay of Islands, on New Zealand's North Island, lies 1050 miles south-southwest of Fiji. Our plan was to sail a course to intercept a point 300 miles due north of there. This plan afforded us a hedge against the possibility of encountering a southwesterly gale that would be dead on the nose if we sailed the direct rhumbline.

Our initial course took us through Kandavu Passage, which rivals the Molokai Channel for pure meanness. As dusk gave way to darkness, *Swan* sailed steadily at six knots, on course, close reaching on the port tack into the northern reaches of the Tasman Sea.

I stood on deck checking the set of the sails with a flashlight and looking over our little ship in our private world. To the south lay the trackless wastes of the great Southern Ocean, stretching unimpeded for thousands of miles to the frozen continent of Antarctica. The constellation Orion, the mighty warrior, dominated the clear night sky. Both Magellanic Clouds were clearly visible—faint, silvery patches that at first glance appear as wispy clouds, but are, in fact, galaxies 150,000 light-years away.

Our progress during the first four days of the passage was erratic, and ended in a dead calm. It turned out to be the proverbial calm before the storm.

The wind came in the early hours of the morning.

At dawn the sky appeared dark and ominous. Thick gray clouds covered the sky from horizon to horizon and the wind continued to increase in force.

React! Furl the main. Run up the trysail. Hatches and ports dogged down tight. String additional lifelines from backstays to stanchions amidships. Foul weather gear stowed close at hand. Fill the thermos with coffee. Check all lashings—the Tasman Sea is cocking the hammer!

The seas continued to build in lockstep with the wind. No longer did the sea look blue and warm. It was an unfriendly steel-gray—cold and forbidding, with wind streaks beginning to appear. Once again our lives would depend on the integrity of *Swan*. Vane was holding the course. His flat aluminum head bobbed back and forth rather comically as he reacted to the forces of wind and sea. I blessed his little mechanical heart and went below.

I marked a DR position on the chart; this was my total navigational effort for that day. Life below was rugged, but it was nearer the axis of the boat's movement and was far less violent than on deck. Most importantly, it was dry!

We were to fight this gale for four days in various stages of exhaustion, and not one unauthorized drop of water entered the boat, which translated to warm, dry bunks in which to collapse. The mate exceeded the expectations of the entire ship's company by preparing two hot meals each day during the storm. The stove was swung fore-and-aft, and a clamping device gripped the pots, allowing the use of most of the cooking utensils. The cook was stabilized by a padded line run from an eyebolt by the sink to a support post near the stove. This provided a secure triangular work area, although the restraining effects of the arrangement elicited a few remarks from the mate about galley slaving. These were easily borne by the skipper as they were accompanied by the aroma of frying potatoes, bell peppers, onions, and garlic. I fell asleep on the cabin sole musing about the engineering obstacles involved in building a totally gimballed boat, and left the mate in charge of problems on the quarterdeck.

At times our course and the eye of the wind were as one. This, combined with leeway, was forcing us off course to the east at the rate of 40 miles per day. The seas had acquired frightening characteristics; they were 20- to 25-foot, steep-faced monsters. Spindrift blew off their curling crests, and every few minutes one wave, larger than the rest, would break aboard with a thunderous crash and sluice along the weather deck, searching for anything poorly secured to carry away. When one of these rogues broke aboard it usually slued *Swan* wildly off to the lee. Sometimes the jib would backwind during this pummeling. If this occurred in less violent conditions we would start the engine and power the bow through the wind and back on the proper tack. No chance of that! The engine could not begin to force the bow up into the shrieking wind with the jib aback. There was precious little enthusiasm for tacking in these conditions, so our solution was to jibe the boat quickly just as the sea passed beneath us. There was a bad moment when the close-hauled trysail and backed jib were at right angles to the wind, especially if the timing was off and we were caught on the face of a wave. When the jibe was completed the jib would fill with a tremendous bang that made me marvel at the strength of dacron.

This experience gave me a new insight into why some clipper ship captains, doing battle with the elements at Cape Horn or some other treacherous place, chose to wear ship rather than tack, even though it cost them time, leeway, and sometimes their reputations.

To windward! An unrelenting, hellish thrash to windward for 72 straight hours, driving south against the gale. Fatigue was our constant companion. Normal shipboard functions became an exhausting ordeal, braced against the pitch and roll.

At one particularly miserable moment while crawling on all fours on the pitching foredeck I saw a frigate bird swoop low near the surface of the water. As I clung to the lifelines in the stinging spray I watched it effortlessly bank and turn in its eternal quest for food, so perfectly adapted to the environment that was so hostile to us. What the hell were we doing here, hundreds of miles from land, with our lives in constant peril, out of contact with the world. I thought of my mother. She can't swim a stroke and is scared to death of the water. How could it be that her son, flesh of her flesh, would choose a life that placed him and his mate in the middle of the Tasman Sea in a violent storm with only a thin skin of fiberglass between them and a watery grave? I laughed to myself in spite of everything when I recalled my mother's words in a letter concerning our ordeal in the storm off California: "I don't know where you get it from. If you hadn't been born at home I would wonder." A blast of green water inundated the foredeck, soaking me to the skin. I went stumbling crawling and cursing back to the cockpit.

On the fourth day the winds began to diminish. We attempted to point higher to gain back some of the westing we had lost, but the turbulent seas would have none of it. Every degree higher increased the pounding correspondingly. We scratched the Bay of Islands as our landfall objective and changed course for Whangarei, a port of entry that could be reached on an acceptable point of sail.

Fourteen days out of Suva we were in the approaches of Whangarei Harbor and the channel that leads to the town basin. We sailed past Hen and Chickens, a small group of islets that lie just off the harbor entrance. It was 1415 hours.

The channel is 14 miles long, and the last two miles are shoal water which must be negotiated between half and high tide. Our timing in regard to tide was perfect; our timing for clearing customs and immigration was a little sticky, as their offices closed at 1700. We wanted to clear in so we could go ashore that evening. The mate had broken free from the galley restraining device and was in no mood to cook. Thus began Swan's race against the clock.

For once the southwest wind was on our side, as the channel bears off to the northwest. With the New Zealand flag and Q flag flying under the starboard spreader and the United States ensign streaming aft, we shot up the channel flying every inch of sail that we dared in a 25-knot wind. The channel is a narrow, serpentine waterway with very few places that one feels free to venture outside its well-defined boundaries. Molly was at the helm while I tended the sheets.

Weariness from our overnight vigil vanished with the excitement of our dash up the channel—past Marsden Point with its field of oil storage tanks; past Snake Bank and into Shell Cut Reach, making a full seven knots. Ease the sheets a bit as we enter Tamaterou Reach—haul them in as we run west past Whangarei Airport in the narrows between Limestone Island and Onerahi. It's now 1545. We head due north at hull speed on Kioreroa Reach, passing huge cranes unloading flat-bottomed barges; we wave to the crews of the tugs and lighters who pause a moment to watch Swan pass with her lee rail awash. As the channel narrows we sail into the lee of a wooded knoll, and the wind shuts off like a water tap. We motor the last mile through the shallow water into the crowded harbor.

Two hours and fifteen minutes after entering the channel, a rather bedraggled twosome made fast the mooring lines at the city wharf in the town basin. We would have dinner on shore that evening. Swan looked smart flying her flags in the late afternoon sun—the first cruising yacht of the season to visit Whangarei.

Whangarei's town basin suffers from what appears

to be a nearly universal problem in the boating world: a lack of mooring space. After clearing in we were required to move the boat, which created a predicament as all the slips were filled and there wasn't room to anchor. Our problem was solved by the Murphys, a New Zealand family living aboard their trimaran, who kindly suggested that we raft up alongside them for the duration of our visit.

We were anxious to see if *Starshine* had arrived at the Bay of Islands. Hitchhiking is fairly common in New Zealand, so we thumbed a ride and were in the Opua post office two hours later. *Starshine* had a large stack of mail waiting for their arrival. We added our note to the pile.

Through the Murphys we quickly became acquainted with several families and received an invitation from one of them to "come round for tea, our place, six-thirty." This was to be our first encounter with the language barrier among English-speaking countries. Tea? We imagined dainty fragile cups from which we would sip with three fingers extended as we took tiny bites from delicate crumpets while chatting about proper things. Before leaving we ate a sandwich to stave off hunger until we returned.

Tea, as we were soon to learn, is the commonly used term for the evening meal in New Zealand, and it is far from dainty. Large roasts of lamb, mounds of potatoes, vegetables, baked bread, and often two desserts are served in farmhand portions. Tea *per se* wasn't even served. We drank coffee with our second meal within an hour.

There were many small boat jobs that we had put off until we reached New Zealand. Cottage industry abounds there, and it's a perfect place to do major or minor repairs to a yacht. It was November first and I was working on deck when I looked up and saw Doug Balcomb striding down the wharf. I scrambled up the ladder and as we shook hands he said in clipped words: "This is *not* Opua."

He and Linda stayed with us for a few days and we

put a major dent in Whangarei's wine reserves as we hashed over our adventures of the preceding eight months. They had been practically adopted by a family in the Marquesas, and were to visit those islands two more times before they finally hung up their cruising anchor for good.

Never before during our voyage did a period of time pass so quickly as the two months we spent in New Zealand. We traveled more than 800 miles overland, a large portion of it by thumb.

We rented a small cabin at the Bay of Islands, that seafarer's haven that had proven to be so elusive to us a few weeks earlier. Yachts were arriving daily from points throughout the South Pacific, seeking protection during the hurricane season. We knew several of the boats from our stay in Hawaii and elsewhere, and it required several parties to hear all the tales.

Our respect for the tenacity of the New Zealand farmer was greatly enhanced when we were invited to spend a few days on a dairy farm. There are no paid holidays there! Twice each day, seven days a week, a herd of mooing, grunting, impatient cows are waiting at the milking shed.

One of our trips through the farm country required five rides, including a short hop on a lumbering relic of a truck hauling hay, to cover 120 miles. At one stop near a farm along the highway we watched a lone sheep dog rounding up 50 or 60 sheep. The objective was to get them through a gate at the far end of a large paddock, and the sheep were firmly against the idea. The dog deftly anticipated the sheep's moves and headed them off, frightening them when necessary with loud barking. When the first sheep went through the gate the rest of them obeyed their basic nature and followed suit. The farmer closed the gate and the dog looked up at him as if to ask, "What's next boss?"

Little Susie Murphy, the girl next door, as it were,

spent many hours on our boat, usually perched at the top step of the companionway ladder. She was an inveterate teller of secrets, always insisting that they be whispered. It made no difference if we happened to be alone at the time. Early one morning she climbed aboard and informed us that it was her fifth birthday and that we were to give her five kisses. "Five kisses!" I replied in mock surprise, "In America we give five spanks!" Shaking her blonde head slowly from side to side in wide-eyed protest she said, "But this isn't America, this is Whangarei!"

On a sunny afternoon we let go the mooring lines on an outgoing tide, bound for Sydney with a stop en route at the Bay of Islands to visit the crew of *Starshine* and to go on a clam digging excursion. Our parting memory of Whangarei was Susie and her mother waving from the deck of their boat as large tears rolled down Susie's cheeks.

There is a small inlet at the Bay of Islands that must be one of the most prolific clam-producing places in the world. In less than an hour we dug enough small steamers to fill a five-gallon bucket. When shucked they filled seven one-pint freezer containers.

For what it was worth, the latest weather reports were favorable. They showed a high-pressure system leaving Australia and moving eastward toward New Zealand. Our paramount desire was to get the Tasman Sea astern of us and into the memory category as quickly as possible. More than 50 boats had turned back a year earlier during the Sydney-Hobart yacht race after tangling with the Tasman. That should tell you something about the place when you consider that those racing fellows seem to enjoy being wet and miserable.

The Tasman Sea was named after poor old Abel Tasman posthumously, and he never had a chance to fight back. It would be similar to having a plague named after you! At least Abel could say that he stumbled onto the infernal place by accident back in the chartless 17th Century. Not us, though. We were simply picking up our anchor in a clam-filled bay and sailing right out there with our eyes wide open. Well, unfortunately there's no way to sail from New Zealand to Sydney without crossing the Tasman Sea.

Our departure from New Zealand was textbook perfect. We stood out north-northwest for 60 miles before making a westward course change, clearing the treacherous North Cape by a 20-mile margin. A relatively shallow area called Wanganella Banks lies 300 miles westnorthwest of the cape. It was on these banks that we came closer to buying the farm than at any other time during the four year voyage.

We had altered our course to visit Lord Howe Island, an Australian possession and port of entry 400 miles off the coast of New South Wales. Our course now ran through the banks, which, on the face of it, was not a problem.

In the early evening of the fourth day of the passage we were well onto the banks when we noticed the sky darken to the southwest. An approaching squall is not sufficient reason to run up on deck and take down the sails. We had been in dozens of them since leaving Portland and our normal routine was to maintain a weather eye and be prepared to reduce sail if necessary.

When the squall hit the usual things occurred: driving rain, confused seas, slatting sails, and the vane steering an erratic course. This disrupting affair usually passed in a few minutes, but not this time. This was a line squall, the forerunner of a cold front. Our heading had changed 60 degrees with a stubborn persistence. Lightning was striking nearby, creating disconcerting crashes of thunder. Standing as far as possible from the rigging I looked up apprehensively at our towering electrical conductor of a mast, beckoning skyward among the thunderbolts.

I sheeted the jib aback and feathered out the main to wait until the wind direction stabilized. As I was securing the tiller an incredibly strong blast of wind hit us from the southwest, the likes of which we had never experienced. In an instant *Swan* was knocked nearly on beam ends; then she righted slightly. Seawater poured over the coaming, flooding the cockpit. I was thrown against the lee lifelines and the tiller pinned me with the powerful leeway force of the rudder. Water continued to pour over the coaming and over me, creating a terrible feeling of panic. Molly stood for a moment, mesmerized at the companionway, then came on deck with the presence of mind to close and bolt the cabin door, which was a full two feet above the cockpit sole—a design feature I highly recommend. The four-inch cockpit drain was preventing the cockpit from swamping completely.

The mainsail was no great threat in its feathered-out position but the jib had to come down fast! I managed to free myself from the tiller. Still the water poured over the coaming. The fiendish shrieking wind was increasing in force. Rain and spume were driven horizontally, making it almost impossible to see. At any moment I expected the mast to carry away under the enormous strain. Molly clung to the tiller as I fought my way forward, half floating along the lee deck, which was awash to the top of the cabin ports. The seawater felt warm compared to the frigid driving rain. I pulled myself up on the cabintop at the mast and released the brake lever on the halyard winch. The jib didn't move an inch. I pulled violently on the sail. Fighting total panic I crawled back across the canted, pitching deck to the winches.

The wrong winch! In the wild confusion I had released the main halyard instead of the jib. The mainsail had not come down because the angle of heel was too great and a good portion of the sail was submerged.

I released the jib halyard and to my everlasting relief

the jib fell like a stone to the deck. Immediately *Swan* regained her balance and had a fighting chance. The mainsail came down as the boat righted and flogged violently as if bent on destroying itself and everything around it, making a deafening noise. That, combined with the bolts of lightning, the flying spume, the icy driving rain, and the shrieking wind, created a scene of indescribable chaos.

I tied a line around the mast and began brailing the mainsail down by spiraling the line around it as I worked aft along the boom. The sail repeatedly tore itself from my grasp, ripping my fingernails. I doggedly wrapped the line until the sail was bound like a wild, subdued animal.

By this time I had become a half-mad Captain Ahab and the Tasman was the great white whale. Draped over the boom, totally exhausted, clad only in my underwear, I shouted at the top of my lungs into the teeth of the gale: "You didn't get us this time, Tasman, you miserable bastard—you never will!" It was absolutely idiotic.

The mate tied the tiller amidships with light nylon line to act as a shock-absorber, and we went below. *Swan* lay ahull, beam-on to the wind and seas. I wasn't at all sure what to expect while lying ahull, but I was very sure I wasn't going to have anything to do with raising any kind of sail.

Molly was quite a sight, standing in the galley, soaked to the skin, wet black hair stringing down, shivering and shaking. My teeth were chattering and my fingernails felt as if they had been torn out by the roots. I poured two large belts of whiskey and we spliced the main brace.

The boat didn't wallow in the troughs as I had anticipated; the force of wind in the rigging kept us heeled in a reasonably stable position. My biggest concern was the possibility of the keel tripping on the face of a sea and rolling us over. I had read a great deal about this aspect of lying ahull. The terrifying specter of the mast passing beneath the surface and water cascading into the cabin, with books and pots flying through the air, was firmly implanted in my brain. It wasn't going to happen to us! If the seas became too threatening we would run off before them.

There is little doubt in my mind that this vividly imagined horror saved us from experiencing the real thing about a year later off the east coast of Africa.

The relatively shallow water on the banks, just over 100 fathoms, was creating a heavy ground swell and making a bad situation worse.

I picked up one of our sailing reference books and it opened automatically to the chapter on storm management. As I read the pages on lying ahull, certain phrases leapt out at me: "A low center of gravity and sufficient ballast to recover from a rollover... capable of yielding to the monstrous force of a breaking sea... built to withstand violent knockdowns." Was *Swan* ready for all of that?

By daybreak the seas had built into steep-faced Tasman specials. They would charge down at us with a vengeance and *Swan* would lift as the sea roared under us.

"Come look at these monstrous seas," I called to Molly, who was in the bunk buried beneath a pile of blankets.

"I don't want to see them."

"You can't just hide from things!"

"Yes I can!"

By midday the winds had diminished enough that we were able to press on under storm sails. I was very pleased with the way *Swan* handled her first experience of lying ahull, and she did it without any help from us, unless one counts worrying.

I obtained our position with two virtuoso sextant performances that, considering the rolling, pitching deck, would have warmed the cockles of Nathaniel Bowditch's heart.

The wind steadily decreased in force in the late afternoon and evening. During the preceding 24 hours we had nearly lost the boat and most probably our lives. We really couldn't fault our seamanship. It was just part of the risks inherent in crossing big oceans in small boats.

The Tasman Sea isn't all bad. It helps forestall any fool notion one might be harboring of sailing around Cape Horn one day. It's a wonderful place in which to acquaint oneself with the most basic instincts of survival, and it did give up three nice albacore and a dorado. I couldn't help thinking this was a crude attempt to beguile us into returning one day so that it could take another shot at us.

The strong plus was that an unpredictable ocean had given us a crash course in heavy-weather management and instilled a confidence in ourselves and our sturdy little ship that had not existed before.

As we sat in the cockpit enjoying one of most pleasant sails we could remember, the sun went down in a sky of blazing orange. In the distance a sea bird was making its final effort of the day to find a morsel of food. It was serene and quiet. No evidence remained of that fearful stormy night, save the gentle scend of the sea.

9

A FRESH NOR'EASTER drove *Swan* comfortably along at six knots with only the reaching headsail poled out. The evening star-fix placed us 115 miles east of Lord Howe Island and neighboring Ball's Pyramid. We were in a perfect position for a landfall. Even at nine knots we couldn't reach the islands before dawn; at our present speed we would arrive in the afternoon. Still, we spent a lot of time on deck during our watches, peering ahead into the moonless night. This passage had been planned around favorable weather forecasts rather than the beneficial phase of the moon, and the net result of this thoughtful, prudent approach was that we got neither.

The morning round of stars fixed our position 30 miles east of the nearest hazard. A light rain was falling when Molly sighted Ball's Pyramid, an aptly named monolith with sheer, craggy cliffs that rise 1800 feet above the pounding surf. It's a weird, towering rock that only a bunch of sea birds could love. Within two hours Lord Howe Island hove into view. We threaded our way through the opening in the reef on the leeward side of the island. Chain moorings are provided for visiting yachts, as the holding ground is poor.

Lord Howe Island is a dependency of the Australian state of New South Wales. Its population of approximately 250 is mainly Australian. The economy is almost totally reliant on tourism, with the chief attraction being its tranquil atmosphere. High kentia palms sway in the breeze, and sprawling banyan trees cover large areas, overhanging into the narrow roads used mainly by tourists riding bicycles.

The island is almost too sedate. We yawned our way through a three-day visit. Our cruising life was running the gamut of emotional peaks and valleys. From violent nights bordering on the brink of death to going to bed with the chickens from sheer boredom.

We were anxious to get moving as the winds were still favorable for the run to Sydney. We wanted to get to the Cruising Yacht Club of Australia and secure a transient berth prior to the return of the yachts in the Sydney-Hobart race.

Three hours out and the island was no longer visible. The fair wind and barometer held steady for the entire passage, yielding effortless daily runs of 130 miles or more. Sunny skies and medium seas. The Tasman Sea was either doing a long overdue penance for its wretched ways, or it has a gentler side that has gone unnoticed by the great majority of the seafaring world.

Sea birds were in abundance. An albatross followed us for three days. It had a seven- or eight-foot wingspan and soared for hours with no perceptible movement of its wings. Numerous frigate birds flew excitedly around the boat, making swooping dives at our fishing lures. The inevitable finally happened. One of the birds hooked a lure with its beak. It rotated through the water like a pinwheel, fouling the other line. By the time I had pulled in the line the bird had drowned and the lines were in a mess that defied description.

The East Australian current sets south along the coast of New South Wales. We attempted to compensate, but ended up approaching the coast five miles south of Sydney Heads. The sun had just set and we hadn't the foggiest idea where to go once we entered the harbor. As unappealing as it was, we felt the wisest plan was to lay off until dawn. We were motoring slowly about 300 yards off the southern head, where great combers were crashing thunderously on the rocky shore, when the engine quit with an abrupt jolt. In a few moments I discovered the reason. We had made the lubberly blunder of not properly securing the port jib sheet in its pocket in the cockpit, and during our little sightseeing tour the sheet had slipped overboard and fouled the propeller. The line was stretched rod-tight, which prevented it from being uncleated and thrown off the winch. The sail was lying on deck in the close-hauled position.

The wind was blowing onshore in a direction about 45 degrees to the shoreline. We were lying with our starboard side beam-on to the wind. If we raised the sail it would fill and drive us headlong toward the rocks with no way of releasing the fouled sheet when we tacked. Tacking would place us in a hove-to position, a move which at best would reduce us to a position of impotence in the face of impending disaster.

We weighed this dangerous gamble as we were being set down on the rocks and certain destruction. The threat had impaired my thinking capacity, but finally instinct provided the obvious solution: I grabbed the razor-sharp knife at the companionway, cut away the fouled sheet, and ran the clew around the mast. Molly took a couple turns on the winch with the remaining sheet, and we hauled up the sail in the backwinded position. For a few sickening moments the bow pointed straight at the rocks as *Swan* fell off to the lee. I put the helm to weather and she wore around until the jib filled on the port tack, allowing us to claw away from those fearsome rocks. For two hours we sailed straight out to sea while we tried to get our nervous systems back in order.

We spent the night holding our position with checks on the depth sounder and bearings on Macquarie Light beaming at us from atop the South Head. Efforts to free the line from the propeller were in vain and I now had two major concerns: First, had the mishap damaged the shaft and strut, and second, how was I going to get up the nerve to dive under the boat to free the sheet in waters notorious for large concentrations of killer sharks— hungry fugitives from the meshing nets?

I told the mate I would dive at dawn. It had a Walter Mitty ring to it. Dawn came; I didn't dive. I had found several reasons for putting it off. Finally, after exhausting all plausible justification for further delay, I put on jeans, a dark sweatshirt, and deck shoes. I wasn't keen on offering up any unwrapped meat, and the clothes also afforded some protection against the cold water.

Tethered by a harness and wearing a diving mask I went over the side. We backed the jib to dampen the roll, and *Swan* was making leeway in the brisk breeze. I lay flat out on the surface looking down into the ominous depths while being pulled along. It suddenly occurred to me that trolling is the way one catches fish, and at that moment I was the trollee! I quickly pulled myself close to the boat and dove under it. The line was wrapped tightly around the shaft with many overlaps. Several dives later I had managed to cut away most of the line and was sawing at the remaining piece when the steering vane rudder swung around and bumped my leg. I nearly had a heart attack!

The transmission was in neutral and I was relieved to see that I could turn the propeller freely. The cold water had gotten to me, and I climbed stiffly onto the steering gear and into the safety of the cockpit, dripping like a drowned rat. Molly handed me a jigger of whiskey (it was 5 o'clock in Reykjavik) and I downed it in one gulp. At 0930 we sailed, slightly chastened, through the high craggy heads, past the thundering surf, into beautiful Sydney Harbor.

A fresh breeze was whipping up small whitecaps in the harbor as we sailed toward the cluster of masts at the Cruising Yacht Club of Australia in Rushcutter's Bay.

Hobie Cats were out *en masse*, skimming around us like flitting water bugs. We were not looking forward to motoring around in a strange place, looking for a fuel dock or some suitable spot to moor, when the problem was solved by a man on the dock who called to us, "You can tie up here, mate!" Thus began a very pleasant period in our cruising life.

Sydney is a cosmopolitan place on a bay that reminded us of San Francisco. The women are quite fashion-conscious, and the younger ones were given to wearing see-through blouses and skirts split to the thigh, which made walking into lamp posts one of the bigger problems I faced while adjusting to life in a foreign country.

Australian men are, by and large, a hardy lot and this trait becomes more pronounced in the remote regions of northern Australia. They like to belly up to the bar, plant one foot on the rail, and quaff down a few—as in the old days of the American frontier. I fell right in with them.

Bob and Gail Rodman, the owners of a large American ketch, *Summer Wind*, and their crew were there. We had last seen this convivial group at a gathering on their boat at Whangarei on what we all assumed to be Thanksgiving Day. No one had an American calendar and there was a question whether we were celebrating the holiday on the correct Thursday. *Summer Wind*'s skipper, Jerry Hood, a large, imposing man with a warm personality, had settled the matter, declaring by the power vested in him: "This is Thanksgiving Day!"

As I recall, the prayer of Thanksgiving included a selfish request that calm weather might descend on the face of the deep, namely the Tasman Sea, for the following two or three weeks. This request was evidently considered too narrow in scope for the general good of mankind and was rejected outright, judging from the bashing the various boats were soon to receive.

It is one of the delights of cruising to enter a strange port and unexpectedly find another yacht with familiar faces. The party had merely undergone a change of venue.

Sooner than I was prepared for it, the need for gainful employment had reared its ugly head. An American I had met at the club was leaving the country, and his job as a carpenter doing renovation work on a group of old town houses was open. He asked me if I could swing a hammer. I told him I was born swinging a hammer.

He arranged a meeting with his boss on the following day; the boss asked me a few perfunctory questions and hired me on the spot. He told me that he liked Americans' attitude toward work and their general competence which, of course, placed me under instant pressure not to be the first American eightball he ever hired.

On my first day on the job he pointed to a stack of lumber. "Do the architrave in the lounge," he said, and went on his way.

I repeated his words slowly to myself: "Do...the ...architrave...in...the...lounge." Architrave? Lounge? I hadn't the slightest idea where I was supposed to be working or what I was supposed to be doing. I feared that the American eightball had arrived. The very one who had entered this world swinging a hammer!

A bricklayer, called "brickies" Down Under, was working nearby. I apologized for bothering him and asked him if he would give me some assistance.

"No worries mate. What can I do for you?" he said as he deftly flicked a trowel full of mortar into a wheelbarrow 10 feet away.

"Where is the lounge and what in the hell is an architrave?"

He laughed and said, "The lounge is right there,"

pointing toward the adjoining room. "Architrave is the trim around the doors and windows."

"Thanks mate," I said, greatly relieved. The molding in the living room! A piece of cake!

Molly landed a job as a waitress at an enigmatic little Italian restaurant in King's Cross, the part of town where working girls work and shadowy things take place. She never really figured out what went on in the back room, but whatever it was had to be creating the cash flow, because the sale of spaghetti and meatballs certainly wasn't. She kept the silver on her tables polished to a luster and occasionally she would have a customer, usually a tourist who had been duped by the restaurant sign. She would dote excessively on these errant diners to compensate for the warmed-over food.

But the pay was regular and the money didn't look tainted to me or to the check-out clerk at the supermarket where we provisioned the boat for the passage north through the Great Barrier Reef.

March, 1979. The cyclone season was nearly over, and it was time to move on. Cape Town, our South Atlantic jumping-off place, was 8500 nautical miles away—a staggering distance when viewed from our five-knot frame of reference. But it was one step at a time. The 1250-mile-long Great Barrier Reef had a habit of exacting heavy penalties from careless navigators. It held our undivided attention. The season was right for the passage. We were counting on fair winds to the Torres Strait.

The East Australian Current rolls along southward at speeds up to three knots—a force to be reckoned with. There are two schools of thought regarding a northbound passage along the coast. One is a rock-hop close in to shore, where the current is almost nil, like the racing fellows do, or go outside the heart of the current. We chose the latter because Vane could handle the

steering chores and we adhered to our South African
sailing friend's dictum: "If it's too far away to see, it's
hard to hit."

On the day we sailed out of Sydney Harbor a southerly was getting up. The rocky faces of the towering
heads were bathed in brilliant morning sunlight as *Swan*
cut through the seas, reaching northeastward with a fair
wind on the starboard tack.

Good progress! By noon the following day we had
crossed the adverse current, dodged several southbound
ships, and were well on our way to our next port,
Mooloolaba, a small coastal prawn-fishing community
500 miles north of Sydney.

We were trading the treachery of the Tasman Sea for
the perils of the reef, and there are many: venomous sea
snakes, sharks of all description, poisonous stonefish,
the frightful sea wasp with its stringy tentacles that
entangle and poison its victims, and unmarked coral
reefs by the thousands.

On the positive side, the Southeast Trades blow
almost constantly, and the Coral Coast bears off to the
northwest; a perfect combination for a sailing vessel.
The weather is delightful, the scenery is spectacular,
fishing is excellent, and the people take pleasure in
making a visitor feel welcome.

Dolphins were out in force. We never tired of their
puffing, leaping, brash visits. On one of these occasions
a dozen or so of them were making their mandatory
diving passes in front of the bow when we startled two
big turtles that were sleeping on the surface. The closest
one reared its head, peered for a moment at the approaching
aquacade, and made a panic dive with its hind flippers
comically flailing the air.

The weather was getting warmer as we sailed north.
At the latitude of the New South Wales-Queensland
border we changed course to close with the land, arriv-

ing at Mooloolaba in time for the annual prawn festival. A spot was made available for us at the Mooloolaba Yacht Club, and we were instantly made welcome.

The prawn festival was similar to a midwestern American county fair. It began with a parade through the town—floats carrying homegrown teenage girls waving blandly at the crowd lining the road in the blazing afternoon sun. Bringing up the rear, surrounded by kids and yapping dogs, was a troop of bagpipers in Scottish kilts, playing highland music. They stole the show.

The prawn reigned. They were prepared in every conceivable way. We ate them until we were stuffed.

I left Molly somewhere between the tug-of-war contest and the "Guess the Shark's Weight" stand, where an ugly black brute that bore lacerations from the meshing nets hung from a wooden tripod. I retired to the bar at the yacht club, where conversation and Brisbane Bitter flowed freely.

The channel leading from Mooloolaba to the ocean was silted in with sandbars in several places. It would have been easy enough to run aground at low tide, even if we hadn't left a channel marker on the wrong side.

"Red Right Returning," the sacred rule memorized by millions of American sailors, got us into trouble. In Australia the channel markers are the reverse of the American system. We knew that, but when the channel made a sharp turn I instinctively went on the wrong side, running hard aground on an ebbing tide. Our efforts to get free were thwarted by the current, which pushed us harder aground with every movement of the boat. We would have to wait for the tide to change.

"Hey Yank, the channel's over here!" shouted a grinning fellow in a runabout. I waved feebly, standing beneath the Stars and Stripes.

We were heeled over a fair degree when it dawned on us that the prawn fleet, in full dress and loaded with revelers, was due to parade through the channel as a culmination of the festival. The thought mortified us. I entertained the idea of striking the colors and hiding below. No! When the fleet passes by we'll sit bravely on the slanted decks, smiling and waving blandly like the girls on the floats.

The Auxiliary Coast Guard came to the rescue in a small boat that seemed to be all engine. They threw us a line, which I fastened to the bow cleat. None of us had much faith in the success of the effort, but when the skipper gunned that enormous engine, *Swan* pivoted on her keel and, to my astonishment, slid off into the channel. The Coast Guard skipper was so surprised that he neglected to throttle down, and the tow line was much too short. He made a panic U-turn to avoid a row of pilings, and we had no recourse but to follow close on his heels. He more or less attempted to run away from us like a horse trying to run away from a wagon. Finally, with our engine in full reverse we stopped without damage to either boat.

They escorted us to the breakwaters, where one of them called out, "There are Coast Guard stations all the way up the coast."

"Thanks," I shouted back, "We'll probably need them!"

They laughed and roared away toward Mooloolaba.

Round Hill Head, a prominent headland, is at the southern tip of Bustard Bay. It was the first place in what is now Queensland that Captain Cook put a landing party ashore. Cook named the bay after the bustard, a wild turkey they shot while on shore. The landing party agreed that the bird was the finest meal they'd had since leaving England.

By the time Cook entered the Coral Sea during his first voyage of discovery (begun in 1768) he had used the names of most of the English lords, admirals, and various potentates who are now immortalized geographically around the world. And so it was that the lowly bustard joined the honored company.

We went ashore at Round Hill Head and climbed the slope where Cook and his men had walked two centuries earlier. Below us *Swan* lay at anchor, alone in the desolate bay that had changed little since Cook's time. In my mind's eye I saw her as the 368-ton bark, *Endeavour*, the sturdy, blunt-bowed, little ship that had risen from her humble beginnings as a collier to carry this courageous team of explorers around Cape Horn, to the frozen reaches of Antarctica, through the perils of the Coral Sea, and back to England. Her round bottom, ideal for careening and accidental grounding, made her an excellent choice for a voyage of exploration, and had most likely saved her from joining the roughly 1600 ships, large and small, whose remains lie scattered throughout the great expanse of the barrier reef.

The more I learned about Captain Cook, the more I admired him. James Cook, that rather dour Yorkshireman, did more to improve the plight of the ordinary seaman than anyone before him and possibly since. He managed to maintain the focus of his mission without exacting unreasonable sacrifices from his men. One can visualize his crew, clambering down ice-laden ratlines with numbed fingers in the frozen Antarctic latitudes, and their reaction to their captain as he stands with his back to the bitter wind and personally ladles a tot of rum to all hands.

Scurvy was almost nonexistent during the voyage because Cook paid attention to the men's diet and their living conditions. A captain's concern for his men was unheard of in those days of press gangs and greedy ship owners, who thought only of profits and had little or no regard for the well-being of the unfortunate souls who were quartered before the mast.

It is difficult to imagine the increasing weight of responsibility that fell on Cook as *Endeavour* progressed through the Coral Sea. He had no idea of the existence of that 1200-mile labyrinth of coral reefs and cays that slowly closes with the land like a gigantic pincer. By the time they had reached 20 degrees south latitude they were well inside the reef. The Southeast Trades blow mightily there, and *Endeavour* wasn't well suited for the windward work necessary to beat back out. Cook and his men would soon be rudely awakened to their dangerous predicament.

For us, the trades materialized at 22 degrees south, giving us excellent daily runs. The anchor was up at first light, and we would sail point to point, checking off the landmarks and hazards until late afternoon, when we'd anchor again, sometimes in a protected bay, but often in the marginal safety of the lee of a windswept cay. More often than not these runs would yield a mackerel or barracuda or some other exotic fish from the teeming sea life in the waters of the reef.

Oysters were in abundance on many of the islands. At low tide we would go ashore with a knife and a bottle of Tabasco sauce, remove the top shells from a cluster of oysters, and eat them as we found them, still attached to the rocks. *Hors d'oeuvres* Great Barrier Reef style! Only a completely inept person would starve to death on the reef.

A few miles east of Cape Bowling Green, a low, sandy spit, lies the wreck of the steamship *Yongala*. In 1911 she was running before 90-knot winds in a tropical cyclone, seeking shelter behind the cape, when she foundered. More than 100 crewmembers and passengers were lost.

It was near there that the shock-absorbing tubing on one of our trolling lines stretched fully out, and *stayed* stretched out. There was something big on the line! Wearing leather gloves I began the arduous task of hauling in a heavy fighting fish while moving at six knots. It flashed bright silver as it burst through the surface of the water and fell backward. The line sang out over the transom and then went slack. Thinking the fish was lost I began taking in the line when it suddenly jerked through my hands. The fish fought a brief but vigorous fight and then abruptly gave up. Molly gaffed it and we hauled it on board. It was a mackerel, over five feet long.

This was a whole lot of fish for two people who were getting a little tired of eating fish. A sentence in the fish species book caught my eye: "The king mackerel has a high commercial value." High commercial value!

"What we have lying here in the cockpit appears to be a large fish, but in fact it is a big night on the town," I said grandly to the mate. "If the wind holds we can make Townsville before sundown. There, the fish buyers buy fish and the champagne flows." I was really warming to the idea despite the mate's rolling eyes.

At sundown we were tied alongside an Aussie yacht at the charterboat wharf in Townsville. A man on board told us the king mackerel was in demand and that we wouldn't have any trouble flogging it off at a nearby take-out restaurant on the waterfront.

I heaved the critter on my shoulder and we walked along the wharf to the restaurant. Several customers were standing at the counter. One fellow did a classic double take when we walked in. Without missing a beat he said, "You'll be wanting chips."

From the kitchen came a short, plump woman wiping her hands on her apron. Her eyes lit up when she saw the fish, and she readily agreed to buy it. There were no scales to weigh it, so nearly everyone in the restaurant got involved in estimating its weight. We settled on a price, and by means of the catalyst of cash our fish was converted into a filet mignon dinner at the pub next door.

North of Townsville the reef becomes at once more

historical and more perilous. Much of the history is centered on the peril. Of all the ships that have come to grief on those dangerous reefs, *Endeavour* is no doubt the most famous. On the night *Endeavour* struck the reef that now bears her name, she was hauling off to the northeast toward the open sea. This would have seemed to Cook to be a reasonable tactic for the night. His decision is fairly solid evidence that he was not aware of the existence of the barrier reef at that point, as his course was leading them into the heart of the coral maze.

As we approached the spot where Cook changed course I tried to imagine what I would have done, faced with the cluster of islands dead ahead as night was falling, and without benefit of a chart. Without a doubt I would have opted for sea room and sailed into trouble.

With a combination of good luck and hard work Cook and his crew managed to patch the hull temporarily and float the ship off the reef after jettisoning her ballast and several cannon.

We sailed near Endeavour Reef and along the route where Cook's men bent to the oars, towing the wounded ship to a small bay on the mainland where Cooktown is now located. We anchored a few yards from the spot where *Endeavour* was careened for repairs.

The now-wary explorer climbed to a high lookout in an attempt to discern the hazards that lay to the north and east. Cook was by no means aware of the full extent of the perilous reef, but a reality was gradually becoming clear to him—it was large and they were trapped.

Cook's first stop after completion of repairs to his ship was at Lizard Island, 18 miles off the mainland. Again Cook climbed a peak, where he "perceived a passage" out of the reef. They passed through this opening, and as it turned out it was nearly their undoing.

On the morning that we left Cooktown for Lizard Island the trades were blasting across those hazardous waters at 35 knots. The wind was on the beam and we flew only the working jib. *Swan* made the 18-mile passage in two hours and forty minutes. I was out of breath from running up and down the companionway, plotting bearings. Our nervous systems required that we hug the leeward side of the upwind reefs so we wouldn't hear the roar of the surf as it spent its fury on the business side of the leeward reefs.

The sun was high and behind us, which was ideal for working our way through the fringing reef into the anchorage at Lizard Island. There is no surge in the bay, but there is a valley between the mountains that allows the wind to blow across the bay unimpeded. This unpleasant aspect of the anchorage forced us to row ashore obliquely to the wind, then drag the dinghy along in shallow water around the bay until it was directly upwind from *Swan*. Stopping the dinghy was the only problem on the return trip.

A sign on the beach had an arrow pointing toward the mountains and "Cook's Look." The hot sun quelled any urge to climb the peak where Captain Cook did his "perceiving."

We proceeded to a tourist resort at the edge of the bay. All that plotting and rowing had made us thirsty for a Foster's brew, one of Australia's better beers. We nearly choked on it when the waitress presented the bill to us. It was definitely not a place for cruising sailors; at least not us.

Endeavour and *Swan* parted company at Lizard Island. Cook went from the frying pan into the fire: About 160 miles north of where they exited the reef, the redoubtable Cook and company found themselves becalmed in deep water, and being inexorably set down on the reef by giant tradewind-generated combers. They were spared total destruction by a fortuitous opening in the reef, through which they eased back into the frying pan unscathed. The relatively calm water inside the reef must have been an incredible relief to Cook, despite the inherent dangers lurking there.

It was in Princess Charlotte Bay that our mechanical troubles began. We were motoring out of a sheltered anchorage in the lee of a large cape at daybreak when a loud hissing noise came from the engine compartment, ending in a dreadful clang and then silence. Silence from the engine compartment; stunned silence in the cockpit; silence from the forlorn gray hills that border that desolate stretch of coastline. There was no doubt in our minds—it wasn't a minor breakdown.

We are not sailing purists who look with disdain at engines. A diesel auxiliary makes cruising in a sailboat much safer and more pleasurable. Ours had driven our refrigeration and electrical generating systems flawlessly for over two years. This was the first engine problem of any account.

An exhaust valve spring had broken, allowing the valve to drop into the cylinder; the piston had then punched the valve through the cylinder head. Remarkably, the piston itself and the cylinder walls were not damaged. The cylinder head, however, was rendered suitable only for service as a dinghy anchor.

Our immediate problem was twofold: one, the freezer was packed full of meat that we had purchased in Townsville for the passage to Africa; and two, it was over 100 coral-strewn miles to Portland Roads, the next settlement where there was a chance of finding some form of communication. Sailing through the reef didn't bother us as much as the thought of anchoring in close to the reefs under sail alone. We were thankful for the time we had spent practicing sailing the anchor in and out.

Three slightly nervewracking runs later we tacked in close to Restoration Island. It was there that the much-maligned Captain William Bligh and his crew of loyalists stopped to forage for food and water after their grueling open-boat voyage from the site of the famous *Bounty* mutiny. Later that day we dropped anchor just off the reef at Portland Roads. There were three houses, no telephones, and the meat in the freezer was beginning to thaw.

In the anchorage with us were some people from Cairns on a power launch. They were in the mining business, there to investigate some coastal land as a potential tin-mining site. We had met them a few days earlier at another anchorage, and they were aware of our engine problem. For business reasons they had chartered a bush pilot to fly them to Cairns, and they obligingly offered to order our repair parts there.

On shore we met Ross and Nita Pope who, with their teenage son and daughter, lived in one of the three houses in this bustling metropolis. The Popes are retired lighthouse keepers and are salt-of-the-earth people. I suggested to Ross that if there were no means to refrigerate our meat, we should quickly plan one of the bigger barbecues in Portland Roads' history. It wasn't a problem. Ross had built a heavily insulated, diesel-powered freezer in the side of the hill behind their house. He stored our frozen provisions and not an ounce was lost.

The isolation of the Pope's home did not deprive them of modern amenities. Their electrical power needs were furnished by a diesel engine-driven generator, and water was supplied by a gravity-fed system from two hillside springs and a rain catchment device. Cooling breezes blew through large shuttered windows in their living room overlooking the bay. In front of the house three towering coconut palms stood at the water's edge, perpetually bent from the nearly constant onshore wind. Papayas, mangoes, and limes grew in abundance and life was good there.

We stayed for two weeks in the roadstead, waiting for the repair parts to be shipped from Sweden, via Cairns, via bush pilot. We filled the time gathering oysters, hunting crayfish on the reef, showing slides of our trip at the Popes' home, and working on magazine articles.

Early one morning we were startled by an aircraft making a deafening low-level pass over the boat. It circled out over the ocean and headed back, now that the pilot had gotten our undivided attention. The plane approached at about 100 feet above the water with its wings waggling. When it passed over us the pilot dropped a transparent plastic bottle with a cloth streamer attached. It landed a few yards from the boat and I scrambled into the dinghy to retrieve it. The plane circled again, and seeing that we had gotten the bottle, the pilot waggled the plane's wings again and shot out over the reef.

In the bottle was a message. Molly, who reverts to a little girl the moment a surprise package arrives, was extremely excited. "Open it! Open it! This is just like in the movies!"

The message read: "Engine parts will arrive at the Lockhart Aboriginal Mission airstrip sometime on June 29, 1979." That is as close to a timetable as bush pilots get.

The mission was located 27 miles inland from Portland Roads. Ross had the mail contract for what must be one of the most rugged postal routes in Australia. He delivered the mail in his Land Rover once each week. We went along with him to see his route and to pick up our parts.

It was an interesting and outlandish 27 miles. We crossed creeks on bridges that were nothing more than two thick timbers spaced apart for the wheels to roll on. The Land Rover was in four-wheel drive for most of the trip, fording streams and churning crab-like up and down muddy red-clay hills. The trip took two hours each way.

The airstrip is the life's blood of the mission and the settlers in the area. It was built by the Allies during World War II, and was used extensively for combat missions during the battle of the Coral Sea.

We had braced ourselves for the bill—not only for the engine parts but for duty and air freight. We were handed a carton not much larger than a shoe box, and found that we hadn't braced ourselves enough. It all came to $640! I clutched my heart and staggered off into the bush among the dingoes and wallabies, looking toward the heavens. "This is the big one—I'm coming home."

Our last deposit to our bank account had been my three weeks' vacation check from General Motors in 1977. After taxes, that sum was very close to the price of the parts. Three weeks of pay wiped out with one punch of a piston!

Molly sat in the stern of the dinghy cradling the parts as if they were the crown jewels. I rowed like a robot, mentally attempting to pick up the pieces of the shattered cruising budget. Suddenly the solution dawned on me—the solution that has stood the test of time for millions of working-class Americans throughout our history when financial setbacks occur.

"We'll take it out of the grocery money!" I blurted out to the mate.

"The grocery money! What grocery money?" she said as she laid the crown jewels in the bottom of the dinghy a little more roughly than I liked. "We've been eating oysters and fish for weeks!"

"Oysters and fish!" I shipped the oars and, counting on my fingers, proceeded to refresh her clouded memory.

"One," I said, "remember the family-size can of Safeway's own brand of extra-hot chili we opened right off Cape Bowling Green near where the *Yongala* sank?" I was pleased to see that it had slipped her mind. I was just at "thirdly" when the mate remarked in a very snippy way that if we were going to New Guinea it might be a good idea to take the big boat. An offshore breeze had been carrying us out to sea. It was rough rowing back, and given the mate's frame of mind, she thought that the water I splashed on her was carefully aimed.

Many hours later the sounds of a living, breathing, diesel came from the engine compartment. Len and Brian, the two mining prospectors, gave us the thumbs-up sign and remarked how the engine "purred like a kitten." Describing the sound that our two-cylinder engine makes as a "purr" was either a case of gross hyperbole or they had been living around mining jack-hammers too long.

On the following morning we were on our way to Thursday Island in the Torres Strait. Our mechanical misfortunes had been greatly assuaged by the warmth and generosity of the people at Portland Roads.

We passed the area of the reef where the *H.M.S. Pandora* ran on the reef and sank while transporting 14 of the *Bounty* mutineers back to England to stand trial. Whatever harsh treatment the mutineers had received under the command of Captain Bligh paled by comparison to the cruelty they experienced at the hands of the master of the *Pandora*, Captain Edward Edwards, who had apparently tried and convicted them in his own mind. Had it not been for one of the seaman opening the overhead hatch of the brig as the ship was sinking, the mutineers would have gone down with the ship to a man. Four of them did anyway, as they were unable to free themselves from their manacles.

The trades were funneling through the channel at Cape York, the northern tip of Queensland, as we entered Flinder's Passage, which leads to Thursday Island. It was a making tide and we fairly flew down the channel.

Thursday Island had experienced its share of economic reverses, and it showed. The islanders hadn't recovered from the decline of their pearling industry, but it didn't appear to dampen their spirits. The island population is comprised of a mixture of Melanesian, Micronesian, and Polynesian races, along with a sprinkling of aborigines from the mainland and a few Australians.

We went ashore in the evening to visit the Grand Hotel. Its grand days had long since passed. There was an aura of decadence about the place that we found appealing. An ornate, grimy latticework enclosed the once-elegant veranda, and the brisk tradewinds served to keep the ashtrays clean on the rickety tables. In a corner of the room three islanders provided musical entertainment: an elderly gray-haired man played a tambourine while two plumpish women with red flowers in their jet-black hair sang and played a guitar and ukelele. They mixed their island songs with American pop music and they were good. I talked with the old fellow in the band, and he proudly told me that he had served with the Torres Strait Light Infantry during World War II when the Japanese forces were in New Guinea, a scant 90 miles away.

We were seated at a table with some Australians, and one of them suggested that we all go to the ball when the pubs closed.

"A ball when the pubs close!" I repeated his words incredulously while looking at our cutoff jeans and thongs.

"You'll be right, mate," he quickly replied. "The dress code is shorts and dress thongs."

We went to the ball.

It was a jam-packed affair. The ticket price included all the food we cared to eat, and the music was provided by a four-piece band that made up for any musical shortcoming with their contagious enthusiasm for fun.

The United Nations could have learned something about interracial harmony at that Thursday Island Friday-night ball.

We were underway at first light. By underway I mean rowing out to *Swan* from the last party on Thursday Island, which took place on an Aussie prawn trawler.

Booby Island and the last coral reef slid over the eastern horizon as *Swan* ran before a fresh breeze into the Arafura Sea. To the southeast lay Endeavour Strait, that broad channel that looks so inviting as one rounds Cape York, but is in truth a shoaling trap that gave Cook another siege of trouble.

Captain Bligh and his debilitated men also passed that way. I could picture Bligh, always the dedicated cartographer, hunched over his journal describing and sketching the coastline, countenance drawn, encouraging the listless men huddled together in the bottom of the open boat. Bligh the enigma, at his best when adversity was greatest and, conversely, at his worst when things were tranquil.

Our passage through the Great Barrier Reef was enlightening and adventuresome; it was also a strain. So it was with no small measure of relief that we sailed into the open sea, bound for Darwin, 700 miles to the west. That evening I wrote the words of the newly emancipated slave in the log: "Free at last, free at last, God amighty we're free at last."

Jim and Molly invited to dinner at a home in Tonga.

Swan *ploughing through Tasman Sea.*

Molly shucking oysters in Great Barrier Reef.

Jim holding king mackerel later sold at Townsville.

Repairing engine at Portland Roads, Great Barrier Reef.

Panama Canal lock gates closing behind Swan.

Using storm trysail to catch water on a squally day.

SAILED AROUND
THE WORLD
YACHT SWAN 1977
1981

Jim and Molly celebrating their circumnavigation.

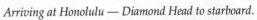

Arriving at Honolulu — Diamond Head to starboard.

Filleting dorado.

Reflection of boat and author in mid-Pacific dead calm.

Homecoming — Swan motoring up Columbia river.

10

A FTER FIVE days of easy sailing we were in the mouth of Dundas Strait, which separates Melville Island from mainland Australia, the shortcut to Darwin from the Arafura Sea. The tide was running against us at five knots and *Swan* was making the same speed. A mountain behind a lighthouse on the mainland created a navigational range that showed us to be sailing in place, with occasional gains or losses. This stalemate lasted for two hours before the tide slackened and the range began to open on the winning side.

We were in Darwin for a week preparing for the long haul across the Indian Ocean. Our plan was to complete all of our business that was farther than walking distance in one day. To accomplish this we rented a Moke, a small, English-built canvas-topped car equipped with only the bare necessities—a glorified go-cart.

It had been many months since I had driven an automobile, and suddenly we found ourselves in a strange little car with the steering wheel to the right and the driving to the left. Molly sounded like a nervous parrot, sitting on the edge of the seat: "Stay left—think left— keep left!" Nearly all of my conditioned reflexes were wrong. The busy intersections were especially tricky, as everything was a mirror image of what seemed correct to us. We ended up giving the right-of-way to anything that moved, despite the blaring of horns behind us.

Our seven-month visit to Australia was at an end.

With our port clearance in order we sailed on the morning tide into the Timor Sea, gateway to the Indian Ocean, and set a course for Christmas Island—a tiny dot on the chart, 200 miles south of Java.

There is an area of light, variable winds that extends several hundred miles west of Darwin. We spent eight days ghosting through those exasperatingly fickle winds. For a 33-hour stretch we sat absolutely dead in the water.

We listened to shortwave radio broadcasts every day—Voice of America, Radio Australia, the BBC, and a Russian broadcast called "Peace and Progress," which was directed at Southeast Asia. Its sole purpose was to decry anything and everything American, particularly the United States dealings with China. The program's commentator was an unctuous, velvet-voiced character who I'm sure would have done well in the used-car business. Nearly everything he said was distorted to the point of being laughable. However, the United States space agency, NASA, was providing some legitimate grist for his mill.

The space satellite, Skylab, had begun to descend toward earth, and NASA scientists had concluded that it would eventually crash in North America. So the Houston Space Center caused the dying satellite to tumble, which altered its rate of descent, making its probable landing site on or near the west coast of Australia. Much better to put Australians at risk than Americans! The Voice of America report carried a lame explanation by a NASA official who said, as if Houston had no choice in the matter, "No one likes to dump their garbage in someone else's backyard." There were a great many Australians who agreed with him.

So that was how it was going to end—demolished by Skylab! We had bluffed our way through fierce gales and sailed through hundreds of miles of hazardous, shark-infested coral reefs, only to be done in by the handiwork of our countrymen. Becalmed in the target zone. Our beautiful *Swan* had become a sitting duck.

I conjured up a mental picture of a red, white, and blue flaming ball of molten metal bursting through our limp and lifeless sails, crashing squarely in the cockpit. But even though I couldn't figure a square root if my life depended on it, I could see that the mathematical odds were in our favor. The Indian ocean covers 28,000,000 square miles and *Swan*'s cockpit measures about 50 square feet. Skylab was likely to miss us. It did.

Then, in the natural order of things, the trades came. It has been my impression that tradewinds begin differently from winds outside the trade belt. A tradewind starts gently, without gusts—a huge ocean of air that slowly and resolutely begins to move with ever-increasing strength. Suddenly everything comes to life. Spirits rise as the sails fill. The boat heels slightly and moves ahead. The almost oppressive silence gives way to the sound of the bow cutting through the water. Gone is the sea's glassy surface, and with it the terrible glare. Close the hatches and ports! We're sailing again!

Thus began a run that would establish a new speed record for *Swan*—478 miles in 72 hours, flying the working jib and storm trysail.

During this run the largest school of dolphins we had ever seen romped by us, taking 40 minutes to pass. Their passing sent thousands of flying fish airborne. One, about six inches long, flew through the companionway and ricocheted off the chart table, colliding with the shortwave radio where it expired in a shower of sticky scales.

Evening star-sights on the thirteenth day of the passage fixed our position 40 miles east and to windward of Christmas Island.

We took in the sails and Vane steered us under bare

poles at two knots. I altered course a few degrees to the north to ensure that we would miss the land if by some miscalculation we were closer than I thought, or if the current were setting us toward the island faster than I had reckoned. The wind was blowing over 20 knots and a heavy sea was running. All this added up to a night of watchfulness. At daybreak the island loomed large and gray, two points on the port bow, 12 miles distant.

Christmas Island is literally the peak of a mountain that rises from the ocean floor so steeply that depths of 100 fathoms can be found 300 yards offshore. A well-protected anchorage, Flying Fish Cove, is on the northwest side of the island.

The island is an Australian External Territory, and its sole economic enterprise is the mining of phosphate. There were nearly 3000 people on the island, two thirds Chinese and the remainder Malayan. There was also a contingent of Australians who managed the operation.

George Clunies-Ross, a dictatorial sort who ran neighboring Cocos-Keeling Island with an iron hand in the 19th Century, periodically made the 500-mile trip to Christmas Island to cut trees for lumber. It was on one of these logging expeditions that the rich phosphate deposits were discovered, and Clunies-Ross promptly exploited them. He built the first road up to the site of the deposits. A Christmas Island postage stamp commemorates the feat, showing the quintessential British colonialist, pith helmet and all, gazing toward the mountain with the inscription: "Road to Phosphate Hill built by G. Clunies-Ross and the Cocos Island boys." It sounded like a Kentucky Bluegrass group.

The mining operation is conducted one hundred percent on the company store concept. But unlike the Tennessee Ernie Ford mining ballad, the labor force does not owe its collective soul to the company store. When we were there, the wages were fair, and the workers had no living expenses other than food and personal needs. Housing, utilities, schools, transportation, and medical and dental care were provided free by the company.

We were given full privileges of the Christmas Island Boat Club. The tiny club does not employ a bartender so everyone serves themselves, signing a chit on the honor system. To the credit of everyone, that unique system on that unique island works.

Our visit to the island happened to coincide with Hari Raya, a celebration of the Muslim New year, marking the end of a month of fasting during daylight hours. As might be expected, the festivities centered around food. For three days the Malayans opened the doors of their immaculate homes to everyone, serving great spreads of their traditional foods.

We were shuttled from home to home and were astonished by the attention we received. An Australian we met during this gourmet's delight belatedly warned us to just sample the foods. We had made the Hari Raya novice mistake of eating too much at the first home we visited, and by the third or fourth stop the sight of a beautifully arranged table laden with spiced prawns, curried fish, rich desserts, and other Malayan culinary specialties had lost its appeal.

The vast Indian Ocean lay before us. It had to be crossed by late October, when, with little warning, the cyclone season can change it from a sailor's reward to a sailor's nightmare.

Swan's 40-inch-wide chart table was covered with nothing but Indian ocean and a few specks of land here and there. Our passage from Darwin had barely put a dent in the seemingly endless miles that had to be sailed to put this ocean behind us—77 degrees of longitude and 4400 nautical miles, to be exact. The entire continental United States, with a fair-sized ocean on either side, could be plopped in the Indian Ocean between Christ-

mas Island and Durban, South Africa, where we intended to seek refuge from the threat of cyclones and to wait
for the favorable time of year for rounding the Cape of
Good Hope. All of these thousands of miles were to be
sailed at approximately the speed of a medium-sized dog
trotting from the living room to the kitchen when he
hears the refrigerator door open.

After a little sleight-of-hand with the calculator I
informed the mate that if we could coax one more little
knot out of *Swan* and average six knots instead of our
customary lackluster five, we could shave 147 hours of
sailing off the passage. I disregarded her flippant and
negative remark that "if pigs had wings they could fly."

Averaging six knots means a lot of sailing at seven
to eight knots—a press to the limit speed for a shorthanded 36-foot cruising sailboat; a speed that places
maximum strain on the rigging at the combined sacri-
fice of safety and the skipper's chances of sleeping
soundly. Besides, 147 hours is only six days, and the
"Dark Continent" wasn't going anywhere.

Port Louis on the island of Mauritius was our next
port of call—2835 blue-water miles from Christmas Island. Our departure from Flying Fish Cove was made in
the company of several curious boobies and some yellowtail
bosun birds that lived in great numbers on the high cliffs
overlooking the anchorage.

The trades were blowing vigorously as we crossed
the wind line, out of the lee of the southern promontory
of the island, into the open sea. Our southwesterly
course, which would take us well south of Cocos-Keeling,
put the wind on the beam, and this called for our
faithful pair of driving mules, the working jib and trysail.

The weather was glorious for four days, then the sky
closed in. Squalls were nearly always visible on the
horizon, paying us wet, blustery visits several times a
day. The wind, at Force 7, fluctuated very little in direc-

tion and intensity, and the sea state built accordingly, creating the largest seas we had ever seen. But we didn't consider them threatening—they were long-period waves, characteristic of the Indian Ocean and kind to the seafarer.

Log entry, September 5, 1979: "Still overcast—reckoning shows us to be 1080 miles west of Christmas Island. Position: Central Indian. Course: Towards Africa."

The cloud cover remained, preventing us from getting a sun-sight for three days. Finally the sun broke through, giving us an opportunity to fix our position. We were amazed to find that after sailing 595 miles without a knotmeter or trailing log we were only eight miles out of our reckoning.

It was summer in the northern hemisphere and the sun was due north at noon. As a person born and raised in the northern part of the world I never really got used to that.

We rigged an awning using the boom and a line stretched from the backstay to a shroud. This made the cockpit a pleasant, shady place and offered some protection from the occasional squall. The boom had been relegated to menial uses of this sort and had little to do with the propulsion of *Swan* now that our westerly course had put the wind on the quarter, and we'd taken the mainsail out of play. The large headsail was poled out to the lee and drove the boat steadily at six knots, often posting 140- to 150-mile daily runs. With the driving effort forward, Vane could hold the course in all but the very worst conditions and I yelled at him less frequently.

It was a replay of that exhilarating run to Hawaii in the heart of the Northeast Trades nearly two years earlier. The constant wind and long swells made it easy to understand why someone had dubbed the Indian Ocean "the sailor's reward." Most likely he was a battered refugee from the Tasman war zone, and after a few days of receiving the pleasant treatment that we were enjoying he had been transformed into a state of gushy euphoria.

Lurking beneath the surface of this pleasant state of affairs was the seductive trap of complacency.

Wearing safety harnesses in fair weather requires discipline, as the danger of falling overboard is slight. However, I believe that if a person falls overboard, unobserved and untethered, on a shorthanded boat in tradewind-generated sea conditions, the chance of survival is about the same as that of surviving a fall out of an airplane. My younger brother was an ironworker doing high building construction, and he summed up the problem of complacency fairly well: "When you get so accustomed to heights that they're no longer frightening, you must stay intellectually afraid, because falling 30 floors is going to kill you whether you are afraid or not."

So we stayed intellectually afraid and wore safety harnesses in fair weather or foul. The value of this decision was made vividly clear, unexpectedly, on a beautiful, sunny tradewind day.

A large cross sea rolled in from the southwest, evidently the aftermath of a southerly gale. Great peaks of seawater were formed by this fractious meeting of southeast and southwest. *Swan*'s bow would deflect sharply to one side or the other when she ran into one of these mounds of seawater, causing Vane to struggle with large course corrections. I was concerned about the possibility of sluing off one of these seas and backwinding the poled-out reacher. I decided to move the clew forward to lessen the chances.

With the sheet eased, I went forward to take up on the foreguy. As I stood looking up at the set of the sail, with my back to weather, my peripheral vision caught a glimpse of a wall of green water breaking across the foredeck, a result of *Swan*'s bow colliding dead-center with one of the heaped-up peaks.

The sea hit me before I could react. In an instant I was knocked over the lifelines. I must have twisted as I fell because I managed to hook my left knee over the lifeline.

A speed of seven knots through the water takes on a whole new meaning when the surface is viewed from about eight inches away while hanging upside down by one leg with your back against the hull. I managed to grab the toe rail with my left hand, then hook my right knee over the lifeline. This greatly relieved the acute pain that the line was causing in the crook of my knee.

Using stomach muscles that hadn't been so callously abused since the days of my stony-hearted basic-training sergeant, I did a vertical sit-up, grabbed the lifeline, and pulled myself on deck.

I can clearly recall my thoughts as I was struggling back on board. They were centered on my safety harness, which I think would have saved me from the final horror of watching *Swan* sail into the distance while Molly slept.

An excruciating pain shot through my left knee as I attempted to stand. It had been twisted during the fall and was the type of injury that wouldn't heal overnight. A long stretch of blue water lay between *Swan* and Port Louis, and my knee hurt with each roll of the boat.

I spent many hours and days lying in the cockpit reading under the awning while my knee mended. Molly attended to the daily chores involved with passagemaking under sail. From time to time I would make a manful contribution to this effort by raising myself up on one elbow and reading the compass, which held steady as Vane steered us die-straight toward Mauritius. I was, however, very generous with advice for the mate. The advice was sometimes poorly received, especially in the area of navigation. In normal circumstances I almost always took the sextant observations and the mate usually worked them out. It was a good arrangement, as my sights were more accurate than hers, and she was less prone to making errors when extracting data from the navigation tables.

She had grown somewhat tired of my cautioning her about the consequences of confusing celestial bodies. This subject nearly always ended in my rehashing the incident in the eastern Pacific Ocean during our first blue-water passage, when the mate observed the wrong star and the resulting fix placed us 20 miles south of Phoenix, Arizona.

During one of her sessions with the sextant I mentioned that she was "waving that thing around like you're shooting skeet." This was not taken as the constructive criticism I had intended. Several hours of silent reading followed while *Swan* ran westward into the sunset on an aging DR.

September 8, 1979—Molly's birthday, the eleventh day out of Christmas Island, an eventful day. It began with my morning ritual of inspecting the rigging and clearing the decks of flying fish. On this morning there was a record 33 fish scattered about.

An albatross had been following us for two days. It became excited as I threw the fish overboard. That's when it discovered the lure on our trolling line. With its wings tucked, it made a lightning dive and a direct hit on the lure.

The last time this had happened I'd made the mistake of pulling the bird in too slowly in an attempt to minimize injury to it, and the bird had drowned. This time I pulled it in as fast as I could, trying not to think of what the double hook must be doing to its mouth as it skipped and bounced over the surface.

When the bird reached the transom I swung it aboard. It was amazingly light for a bird with a six-foot wing span. It looked very dead.

The hook was stuck in its beak, and miraculously had not damaged any soft tissue. I dislodged the hook and turned the bird upside down, gently squeezing it. It regurgitated a large quantity of water. Three times I did this and each time more water was expelled.

Suddenly it startled us with a loud *AWK*! It tried to spread its great wings, which were so majestic soaring above the waves and so ungainly in the cockpit, catching on lifelines and rigging. We carefully folded its wings as it sat there with a dazed expression. It began to halfheartedly preen its feathers. I suggested to Molly that she administer mouth-to-beak resuscitation should the bird begin to fade away.

Now that the crisis was apparently over we took the opportunity to examine the albatross closely. It was a marvel of strong, light construction. The bird seemed detached from its unusual circumstances and didn't seem to mind our examination. The dazed look, combined with disheveled neck and head feathers, gave it a comical appearance that reminded us of Daffy Duck after one of his harebrained schemes goes awry and an explosive device blows up in his face.

As the bird recovered it grew restless and we were afraid it would injure its wings, which would amount to a death sentence.

I picked up this wild but gentle creature and it stood with its webbed feet in the palms of my hands. The wind beneath those outstretched wings lifted it, and it soared in an upward turning arc, finally settling on the crest of a sea about 100 yards away. As we drew away we could see the bird spreading and folding its wings, preening itself, and going through what appeared to be an albatross version of a preflight checklist. Daffy of the Indian Ocean was ready for his next adventure.

We were practically catching fish at will. Scarcely were the lines back in the water when a bright, 12-pound yellowfin hit. Molly decided that baked fish would be the centerpiece of her special birthday dinner.

With the leeward ports open and the quartering wind ramming down the companionway, the oven was once again a usable piece of galley equipment. The fish was too large to fit in the oven, so I modified it at some cost to artistic presentation.

We had recently learned that citrus fruit wrapped individually in aluminum foil will keep for long periods without refrigeration. Lemons are considered indispensable when preparing fish on board *Swan*, and we had sailed out of Flying Fish Cove with a storage net full of lemons and limes wrapped in foil like a cluster of silver Christmas tree ornaments.

I was retrieving a bottle of South Australian wine from a cockpit locker when I glanced over the weathercloths and was startled to see a large freighter running parallel to us less than a quarter of a mile to leeward. It was the first ship we had seen for 11 days.

I switched on the VHF radio and caught a European-sounding voice in mid-sentence: "...calling sailboat on my port side." I answered. The captain, a Dutchman, apologized if he had startled us. His ship was transporting wheat from Australia, bound for Odessa on the Black Sea via Suez. He had altered course to have a closer look at this small sailing yacht so far from land.

He offered to send a cable for us, and we accepted. It was sent to our friends the Schmiels, in Portland, and included the latitude and longitude where the signal originated. This caused a bit of a surprise in Portland, as we were nearly in the geographical center of the Indian Ocean at the time.

We sent two messages that day; both were received. The cable was sent at the speed of light; the other by perhaps the slowest means imaginable—an empty wine bottle from Molly's birthday dinner. We set the bottled message adrift to follow the whims of the current. It would travel 2500 miles in 230 days and add another dimension to our lives.

Our navigational routine in mid-ocean, far from the threat of land, required very little time or effort. It generally consisted of a 1000 hours sun-sight, crossed as a running fix with latitude by the sun at noon, or a noon latitude crossed with the moon if it were visible. The latter did not require the wait between sights, and got the quartermaster work done quickly.

With the noon position posted on the chart and entered in the log, navigation was not thought about again until the following day, except for the compass heading and a general awareness of our average speed.

To some, this might seem a rather nonchalant attitude toward the way of the ship. It's not. Near land the rules change.

At noon on September 7th there were 11 inches of barren ocean on the small-scale chart between *Swan* and Mauritius. During the ensuing 24 hours we sailed a good run of 146 miles, and at noon on September 8th 10 inches of ocean separated us. Not exactly an imminent threat.

On the 20th day of the passage the proximity-of-land jitters had acutely set in, and could only be cured by morning and evening star-sights in addition to the usual noon fix.

Mauritius is a comparatively safe, easy landfall when approaching from the east. A spherical mound, appropriately named Round Island, is the first manifestation of land, easily distinguishable from the sharp-peaked mountain range on the main island.

With great reluctance we tied alongside a rough concrete wharf near a motley group of rust-streaked fishing trawlers, rafted seven or eight deep, pumping foul liquids into the polluted harbor. Our first and lasting impression of Port Louis was filth—not superficial litter but long-standing, built-up, rat-breeding filth.

Out of pure necessity we stayed the night, taking the precaution of putting screens over the ports and hatches to ward off roaches and rats. Early the next morning we sailed 10 miles north to the more habitable environment of Grand Baie.

In a general sense, most of the sailing on a circumnavigation takes place in the part of the world between latitudes 35 degrees north and south of the equator. Tropical cyclones occur principally within these boundaries. Therefore, a cruising yacht must look for shelter or be well out of the danger zone during the cyclonic period.

At first we viewed this restriction of movement as an unmitigated nuisance, but as time passed we realized a hidden benefit of the regulatory effect of the seasons. That is, cruising yachts tend to congregate at certain ports that can accommodate them during the dangerous season, and this results in the formation of an informal cruising fraternity. Friendships that might never have developed otherwise are formed during these static periods. Durban, South Africa is a logical haven in the western part of the Indian Ocean, and Mauritius is a normal stop en route. Yachts flying flags from all over the world were arriving daily at Grand Baie—some we hadn't seen since as far back as Fiji and New Zealand. Many tales to be told.

The anchorage at Grand Baie is excellent. It's large, fairly shallow, the holding ground is good, and there's a nice landing in front of the Ile de France Hotel.

We found an open space and dropped the hook near the yacht *Tina*, from Massachusetts. We soon met the owners, Walter and Vance James. Vance was sitting on the cabintop with a hand-cranked sewing machine, surrounded by their tattered genoa which had blown out during their passage from Darwin. Later we would have some great times and adventures together in South Africa.

The 14-mile, 45-minute bus ride to Port Louis afforded some unusual sights: Fields of sugarcane stretched for miles in all directions. Huge piles of black volcanic rock that had been cleared from the cane fields dotted the countryside; mute testimony to the back-breaking labor performed in bygone days by slaves under French colonial rule, and later by indentured laborers from India.

Oxen with drooping heads, pulling two-wheeled carts piled high with stalks of sugarcane, plodded along the narrow road. The beasts were driven by listless men whose facial expressions seemed to match that of the oxen—absolute boredom.

The bus rumbled and honked its way into the heart of the market district of Port Louis, where we jumped off and joined the throngs on the sidewalks. Immediately we were besieged by Indian sidewalk peddlers hawking cheap jewelry, wristwatches, and sundry junk—reminiscent of Suva, but these peddlers were more aggressive. I shifted my wallet to my front pocket. As we crossed the narrow, littered street, a huge rat scurried brazenly along the curb among the vendors.

We entered a complex of dingy old buildings that made up the meat and poultry section of the market. Several Indian men stood behind a long table; some held meat cleavers, all were chattering like barkers at a carnival sideshow. The table was covered with thousands of cleaver dents, which were filled with gray, rancid fat. There was no evidence of refrigeration. The meat lay on the filthy table and was covered with flies. As we walked along the table, feigning shopper's interest, a tall, sharp-featured man with dark brown glistening eyes and gold-capped teeth grabbed up a piece of warm, slimy beef and held it out toward me. Several dozen flies that had been feasting on it had to look elsewhere for nourishment as he flopped the revolting slab over and over while extolling its superior quality. I shook my head and gave Molly a nudge as she seemed to be rooted to the spot. "See anything nice for supper?" I said, as we walked outside.

I had an unfortunate need to visit the public facilities, which stretched the euphemism "rest room" well beyond the breaking point. It was a shock to what I thought were my hardened senses. I managed to hold my breath for the entire time, risking brain damage rather than inhaling the putrid air of that vile place.

On every street were pitiful old beggars, some crippled, some just old and withered. They would sit or crouch on the sidewalk with their talon-like hands held out beseechingly, staring with sunken eyes at the stream of people passing by. They were for the most part ignored.

The fresh-vegetable market was the only saving grace of that part of the city, as far as we were concerned. A superb selection of fruits and vegetables were available at very reasonable prices. The produce we bought received three washings before it was taken on board the boat.

Grand Baie was a lovely stop. It was an anchorage without problems, full of interesting and fun people. We had made the passage across the central Indian Ocean without building up the usual long list of jobs to be done in port; there was just one repair to be done: A locking device on the wind vane had broken early in the passage and had been temporarily replaced by a now-rusty pair of vise grips. The repair required two trips by bus across town to the Mauritius Technical School, where the students welded the stainless steel parts I had fabricated from raw materials we carried on board.

The rest of the repair was made fairly simple with the help of a vise I had mounted on a wooden base that could be clamped firmly in the cockpit, and a 12-volt drill powered by the boat's batteries. These two tools were the heart of the "shop" on board *Swan*. When the repair was completed we were able to do as we pleased for the remaining two weeks of our stay.

Walter James, on *Tina*, had a long list of jobs facing him and was amazed at our leisurely activities. I lorded it over him at every opportunity, but he managed to even the score by winning every one of our dinghy-sailing races across the bay to check the mail.

Fifteen hundred miles of Indian Ocean still to cross. Our plan was to give Madagascar a wide berth—at least 150 miles. We had heard negative reports about the treatment of foreign yachts by officials of Madagascar's government, and we weren't inclined to take any unnecessary risks.

After a morning spent clearing port, *Tina* and *Swan* sailed in tandem out of Port Louis on a southwesterly course.

It soon became apparent that the steady Southeast Trades that had borne us so effortlessly across this great ocean were giving way to the variable winds that fringe the tradewind belt. Three days of fickle winds found us dead in the water 300 miles into the passage.

Tina and *Swan* lay motionless, five miles apart, under the relentless blazing sun.

Our radios were tuned to a talking channel and I described to Walter in detail the elaborate, and fictional, breakfast Molly was preparing on our luxury yacht: pheasant under glass, hollandaise sauce, and several other outlandish entrees. For emphasis I would utter asides to Molly for Walter's benefit: "You pluck a pheasant just as you would a chicken." As if she knew how to pluck a chicken.

Suddenly the stillness was shattered by a loud, whooshing roar. We jumped on deck in time to see a whale, perhaps 35 to 40 feet in length, about 50 yards from the boat. It submerged and swam under the stern, surfacing a short distance away. I went below and called *Tina*. We had read accounts, some rather dubious, of whales attacking boats, but the possibility existed and I wanted Walter and Vance to know our situation.

Walter's mind was still on the fictitious breakfast, and when I told him about the whale he said, "Pluck it just as you would a chicken."

"Walter! I'm serious!"

I don't think he believed me until I showed him a photograph of the whale in Durban.

The whale made two more passes. The last one appeared threatening. The attack stories were rapidly gaining credibility. This huge black animal swam rapidly on the surface straight at the cockpit. At the last second it dove, rolling on its side as it glided beneath the surface. We hung over the lifelines staring at a huge eye staring back at us as it passed under the boat, barely missing the rudder. Apparently it was just curious. It never returned.

For five days we sailed westward through the variables. Now the wind comes from the east; now it veers north and freshens—but wait, it's probably a fluke—it seems to be building. Hank on the working jib, *Swan* moves smartly ahead—then the wind falters and dies. Variables! The sails slat, sail-slides rattle; nothing gets on my nerves more. Bring in the fish lines, take down those flapping rags—it's hopeless! We go back to our books—Africa can wait another day.

Strong tradewinds in the Indian Ocean create the great trade drift, which moves westward, dividing at Madagascar. The northern stream strikes Africa's east coast, where it splits again, with a portion of it moving southward and creating the Mozambique Current. This current reunites with the southern part of the great trade drift, forming the mighty Agulhas Current, which is strongest at the 100-fathom curve. The 100-fathom depth ranges from eight to twelve miles offshore, following the contour of the coastline fairly closely from Durban to East London. It is also the edge of the continental shelf, which drops off precipitously.

Our plan was to stay north of the rhumbline to avoid being south of Durban in the heart of the southerly setting Agulhas stream. I was pleased with the progress we were making across the channel. We were 20 miles north of the rhumbline, about 180 miles from Durban, when the northeast wind began to fade.

Molly had become the watchdog of the barometer ever since the hammering we received in the Tasman Sea. She was forever tapping it and setting the monitoring hand. As night fell she announced that the barometer was practically in a free fall. The wind stopped.

I remembered a conversation I had one evening at the Grand Baie Yacht Club with a South African fellow. We were discussing weather on the African coast. He said, "When the barometer drops rapidly, then levels off, and a northerly wind begins to weaken, watch out for a strong sou'wester. A buster can be on you in a flash," he added.

A few pats of rain fell. There was still almost no wind, but it was coal black. An old sailor's ditty came to mind: "If the rain comes before the wind, you'd better get the top'sls in."

The barometer leveled off at 990 millibars. Down 20 points in as many minutes. I didn't like anything about this. Let's get those sails down!

Scrambling on deck we took in the jib and lashed it to the lifelines. We spiraled a line around the mainsail, securing it to the boom, and dogged down everything that could be. Not a minute too soon! The buster hit with tremendous force. An instantaneous 50-knot wind out of nowhere. I mentally thanked my South African pal for his sound advice.

From our earlier experience I was confident in *Swan*'s ability to lie ahull. But there were factors in this instance that increased the risks. My primary concern was that the strong current, running in direct opposition to the gale, could create steep-faced, short-period seas—the arch enemy of a small craft. My other concern, though a lesser one, was that we were in a channel. It was a large channel, but it wasn't the same as being in the open ocean, where land could not possibly join forces with the wind and sea to wreak destruction on the struggling mariner.

The gale-force wind took very little time to build the seas to the point where I was concerned about the possibility of tripping on the keel, burying the leeward rail, and rolling over. In nearly all the reference books I had read on coping with storms at sea, there was a general agreement that when gale-force winds blow in opposition to a strong current, heaving to or lying ahull entails unacceptable risks. This left scudding, or running off, as the only viable option in my view.

Riding to a sea anchor was a theoretical option, and I stress theoretical, as somewhere at the bottom of the Indian Ocean, in 15,000-plus feet of water, lay *Swan*'s sea anchor. I had given it the deep-six to preclude me or anyone else from streaming it from the bow in an attempt to ride out a storm at sea.

It was purchased long before I realized the enormous strain that a spade rudder and self-steering gear is subjected to during a sudden powerful surge of sternway, or the vulnerable position in which a boat is placed when its natural buoyancy is negated by a sea anchor holding the bow down, thus allowing seas to break on board. There may be instances when a sea anchor would be the perfect solution in storm conditions, but I have no idea what they might be, and I am blissfully happy in my ignorance.

The decision to run off was reached moments after my sailor's gut sent an urgent signal to my brain during a disconcerting slide down the face of a giant rogue.

We started the engine and headed off downwind, taking the seas on the quarter about 15 degrees from square with the wave crests. This angle was about right, as the boat heeled slightly, presenting her rounded hull to the seas and creating additional freeboard. It also allowed sufficient helm response to prevent broaching.

The risk inherent in running off in severe conditions lies in too much boatspeed, which creates the danger of planing down the face of a sea, burying the bow, and having the following sea lift the stern and pitchpole the boat end over end.

Boats have survived pitchpoling, but our mentalities demand that things this calamitous can only happen to someone else. The thought of having it actually happen to oneself is too horrible to contemplate—like being in an airliner crash or being recalled into the army.

The wind was a howling gale and *Swan* was far more eager to run before it than I liked. The mast, rigging, dodger, and weather cloths were offering too much windage. Our spirited entry into the troughs was causing me a great deal of anxiety.

I recalled a remark by a weather-beaten seadog in a pub at the Bay of Islands: "Everything that you've ever heard about the currents and storms around the Cape is probably true; it's difficult to exaggerate them. You must watch out for the giant rogue that will make the hole-in-the-sea that can swallow you up." He'd laughed and quaffed down another New Zealand bitter.

A hole in the sea...I was beginning to understand the real possibility of such a thing. That carefree evening in New Zealand now seemed a long time ago.

It was imperative that we decrease boatspeed. While Molly steered I groped through the lazarette and hauled out 300 feet of half-inch line. I tied one end to a stern cleat and looped it out behind the boat. When it began to create a drag I wrapped the line once around a sheet winch on the opposite side of the boat and payed it out, cleating off the bitter end. The boat slowed one or two knots, which helped psychologically as much as in reality.

If need be, I would unearth the Big Gun from the forepeak. For more than two years we had carried an old Toyota tire to serve as a drogue. It was always regarded as the ace in the hole that would one day save us from destruction—a comforting thought that made the storage problem it created tolerable.

But it never came to that, then, or at any time during the voyage. Two years after this stormy night in the Mozambique Channel, in a frenzy of boat cleaning at the safe and tranquil houseboat moorings in Portland, from whence we had tentatively set out to points unknown four years earlier, the tire joined the miscellany headed for the rubbish bin. As I drove away from the dumpster behind a supermarket, I saw in the rearview mirror the once highly valued tire protruding out of the bin. It was perhaps the only Toyota tire in the world to have crossed every degree of longitude under sail, and it now lay ignominiously atop the rotting vegetables.

The fierce wind diminished sharply with the rising sun, and the seas began to lose their mean characteristics. With the threat of disaster past, we were suddenly aware of how famished we were after some 10 hours of being bashed about. For most of those hours the unpleasant feeling in the pit of our stomachs had little to do with hunger. The mate cooked a lumberjack's breakfast while I got the boat back into sailing order and pointed it toward Durban.

A benefit of our ordeal in the gale was that we were now well north of Durban in perfect approach position. Timing was the problem. We would arrive after dark. For the first time in our cruising experience I felt that the risk of entering a strange port at night was far less than the potential danger involved in standing off in the unpredictable conditions of the African coast.

A panorama of lights illuminated the sky as we closed with the coast in the approaches to Durban Harbor. We were guided to the harbor entrance by a large signal light on a high bluff. I contacted the harbormaster by radio and he kindly dispatched a harbor police launch to escort us to the quarantine buoy.

It was after midnight when we settled wearily into our bunks. The pressure was off. Forget the barometer; no bracing against the roll, no ships, no current. It was still and quiet. The Indian Ocean was behind us. Ahead lay the challenge of the great Southern Ocean, around the Cape of Good Hope. But like Scarlett O'Hara, we would think about that another day. Beside me was my wife, who had followed me across 18,000 miles of rugged ocean from our home half a world away. "Africa," I said. "We're in Africa. Can you imagine that?" There was no answer from the mate—she was already asleep.

11

S *WAN* EASED her way among the cluster of foreign yachts rafted up alongside the international dock, as it was called, in front of the Point Yacht Club, nestled in the heart of Durban. On the dock a man with a close-cropped beard watched us approach. He was Bob Fraser, past commodore of the club and now a liaison between the club and visiting yachts. "Welcome to Durban," he said as we shook hands.

Snug in her berth among the press of yachts, *Swan* began a two-month period of idleness, during which time we attended to boat maintenance that we had postponed until we reached this major port.

Testing dye revealed hairline cracks in two swaged terminals on the standing rigging. We replaced all of the standing rigging with larger-size wire, using removable terminals with coned compression inserts.

The plow anchor and chain rode needed regalvanizing after too many encounters with coral heads. The company that did the work also transported the chain, all at a very reasonable price.

But it could never be all work in Durban. The tempo of our social life increased daily, like Sydney all over again. After so many months of sailing in rough and remote regions, and crossing huge expanses of blue water, we were ready for some of the amenities that a modern city and a hospitable yacht club have to offer.

Finances (usually the lack of them) governed to a

great extent what the majority of the cruising people did with their time in port, ourselves included. The Point Yacht Club had one outstanding plus—it was affordable. Never before had we seen so many crewmembers of visiting yachts dining out. There were superb curry dishes, seafood delicacies, and good wines, all graciously served by Indian waiters in the club dining room.

In addition to the main lounge there was a men's bar....

A men's bar is commonplace in private clubs in South Africa. Women aren't allowed in these male watering holes, pure and simple, and it isn't given much thought.

Now this concept did not set well with certain ladies on the visiting yachts, and I never really understood why. If there had been a women's bar or lounge on the premises, wild horses couldn't have dragged any of the men's bar denizens in there.

I believe that from time to time, most men need to be in the company of men; a bunch of the boys shooting the breeze, telling a ribald story or two, and generally enjoying the camaraderie. But it was a bitter pill for the liberated ladies to swallow. It was the unspoken, unwritten words; that tacit understanding that women were not welcome, that bothered them. I sometimes wondered how they abided the existence of a men's room!

Molly does not worry about such things. Therefore, I came away relatively unscathed from my periodic visits to that bastion of male chauvinism. However, I hasten to add that she was not above joining in an underhanded scheme, hatched by the cabal of wronged women, of sending a steady stream of their bar and *hors d'oeuvre* bills into the men's bar for settlement by their respective spouses. The tabs were borne by a blue-coated waiter who would politely say, "Sir, the missus," while presenting a tray bearing the check. It got so that the

mere sight of a blue coat could effectively quash a
delightful rendition of "It's a Long Way to Tipperary."

News from the United States was becoming more
and more disturbing. The Durban newspapers were giving front-page coverage to the Iranian takeover of the
American embassy in Teheran. We read, tight-jawed,
about the Iranians' flagrant attempt to blackmail the
United States government. There were bleak accounts of
escalating trade deficits, primarily caused by staggering
expenditures of petro-dollars, which fueled inflation and
upward-spiraling interest rates. All seemed to be working
in concert to destroy the U.S. economy. The American dollar, heretofore the symbol of economic and political strength, was locked on an unimpeded downward
plunge that came home with a jolt each time we cashed a
traveler's check. "The United States dollar dropped
again," the teller at Barclays would say almost apologeti-
cally as she exchanged our money at the declining rate.

One afternoon I strolled into the men's bar, where
Bob Fraser was holding court. In the course of the
rambling conversation he bluntly asked, "What's happening in America? What's the problem over there?" I
was stumbling over the question when an older fellow, a
regular with high seniority on the corner stool, interrupted
me with another question: "Which one of the presiden-
tial candidates is best for America—Kennedy? Carter?
That Hollywood fellow?"

"I'm the wrong guy to ask," I replied. "I voted for
Nixon twice." It got a laugh and I was off the hook on
the first question.

It occurred to me that perhaps Molly and I were
fiddling while Rome burned, sailing around the world,
spending our dwindling reserves of weakening dollars.
Well honey, grab another handful of that Monopoly
money and let's go to the club for the Sunday afternoon
buffet.

Cocktail hour conversation inevitably touched on rounding the Cape of Good Hope. It was in the back of everyone's mind, like approaching final exams. This apprehension was further kindled by the arrival of a battered Dutch yacht that had been rolled over in a storm in the Mozambique Channel—either the same storm that we had been in, or one following close on its heels. She had been lying ahull and apparently tripped on her keel while sliding down the face of a giant roller. She was dismasted and everything on deck was demolished or carried away. The electronics were all knocked out, and to round out the disaster the propeller shaft was bent, probably by an entangled piece of rigging attached to the mast that had been cut away.

The captain, whom we had met at Grand Baie in better times, used the one spar he had left, the spinnaker pole, to construct a first-class jury rig. The boat had limped across the channel into Durban under her own power.

It was all quite sobering.

With Vance's help, we pried Walter away from his myriad boat projects and prepared for our great safari to the Umfolozi Game Reserve. Instead of employing the traditional troop of strong young men to carry the gear on the hot, dusty trek, and hacking and slashing our way through the bush country, we rented an air-conditioned automobile, loaded it up with groceries and several flagons of wine, and set out for the heart of Zululand on a modern highway.

Much to our surprise, nearly all of the land visible from the highway was under cultivation. Contour-planted rolling hills undulated down into lush green valleys. The soil was rich and fertile, producing bumper crops of sugarcane and maize.

Groups of round-domed huts dotted the countryside. These *kraals*, arranged in patriarchal pecking order, are the age-old homes of the Zulu. The *kraals* have a beehive configuration, and are constructed from long, dried fibers interwoven through saplings that come together at the top to form the dome. There are no windows and only one door, approximately three feet high. To enter the hut it's necessary to crawl or duck-walk, which places the visitor in a vulnerable position—a throwback to the days of the tribal wars.

Along the roadside Zulu women carried heavy loads balanced precariously on their heads. We were astonished at the enormous bunch of green bananas that one stocky woman, about 50 years old, carried on her head for more than a mile up a slope to the highway. It was all Walter or I could do to lift the bunch, which elicited great merriment among the women observing us.

At Umfolozi we rented small bungalows that were clean, comfortable, and inexpensive. Zulu cooks prepared and served our meals twice each day from the food we had brought with us.

The concept of the game wilderness is straightforward: It's the animals' domain; you enter it at your own risk. The "own risk" part was foremost in our minds as we drove into the game area on hard-packed gravel roads.

During our two days there, we saw skittish impala, families of baboons, huge rhinos, kudu, giraffe, wildebeest, zebras, warthogs—and a pride of lions led by a huge shaggy-maned male with a bloody gash on his face. He glowered menacingly at us through the branches of a tree 50 feet from the car. The lions reigned supreme.

As we were driving back to the bungalows, two large rhinos thundered out of the brush and ran parallel to the road alongside the car. Walter stayed even with them while I attempted to photograph the beasts. We were blocking them from crossing the road, which wasn't setting too well with the nearest one, so we stopped. They crossed the road, whereupon the angry one wheeled around, lowered its massive head, and prepared to charge. Instead, we charged—away—as fast as a scared Toyota can go.

In all, we covered more than 500 miles of South African countryside.

It was December; summer on the cape. The ferocious winter busters were moderating, and conversely, northeasterly winds were becoming more frequent—the perfect winds for rounding the Cape of Storms.

I talked to several yachtsmen who had sailing experience racing, cruising, or making yacht deliveries on this rugged coast. They helped put the cape passage in perspective and sorted out the myths. By melding this firsthand information with the recommendations and cautions gleaned from *South African Sailing Directions* and *Ocean Passages For the World*, we were able to formulate a plan for doubling the cape.

We sailed out of Durban Harbor on a rising barometer and favorable weather forecast into the heart of the Agulhas stream. A fresh easterly pushed us at six knots, and with a fair current of four knots we were making an astonishing 10 knots over the bottom.

On the evening of the following day we were 90 miles north of East London, a giant leap down the coast. The continental shelf, called the Agulhas Bank, was roughly at the 100-fathom curve. We were four miles outside of it to take full advantage of the current. The coastal mountains were rapidly slipping past. I was willingly spoiled by such effortless speed and progress. We're flying! Big deal, this cape! The South Atlantic is just around the corner.

My reverie of unbridled optimism was interrupted by the familiar tapping of fingernail on glass down below. The voice of the barometer announced that trouble was brewing, and a glance at the southern sky confirmed the warning. At the 1000 millibar level I turned the boat due west and ran straight for the relative safety of the bank.

We quickly dropped the main and hoisted the storm trysail. From out of the southwest, across the surface of the water, came a stampede of white horses. White-crested wavelets were being formed by the wind and current almost instantly. We eased the jib and trysail sheets to spill out the initial blast of wind. With a whistling roar that was accompanied by the simultane-ous crack of both sails filling, the buster hit. *Swan* heeled sharply, rounded up, then took off like a scared rabbit straight at the coast.

By the time we had reached the bank short, steep seas were forming. Everything seemed to be happening at double or triple time. The current slows markedly on the bank—a fortunate circumstance that changes the rules of the game from life-threatening to extremely uncomfortable.

We hardened the sheets, pointed higher, and pre-pared, if that is possible, for a night of thrashing to windward in conditions that we didn't understand very well.

At 40 fathoms, approximately four miles offshore, we changed to the starboard tack. Our plan was to stay between 40 and 70 fathoms, changing tacks every 40 minutes or so. The depth sounder was more useful on the shoreward tack than on the seaward leg, because the pounding we took as we neared the edge of the bank was notification enough!

It was a long night of fitful catnaps, making up to East London in the eye of the wind. The coastline was no longer zipping past. Bearings taken on the powerful Cape Morgan navigation light seemed as though they would never change. Four hundred miles of treacherous coastline still lay between *Swan* and the southernmost tip of Africa, Cape Agulhas—the corner that the South Atlantic was "just around."

Sunrise found *Swan* alongside the wharf at East London, near a railroad bridge that had real steam locomotives chugging over it. South Africa's large coal reserves had made the resurrection of steam engines a viable option for dealing with the soaring price of oil on the world markets. We hadn't seen steam-driven locomotives for three decades, and I would have liked to keep it that way. In addition to belching black, sooty smoke that settled on everything, the engines would huff and puff rusty flakes off the bridge girders, and these, too, drifted down on *Swan*. The particles united with the salt residue on the deck, creating rust stains in the nonskid surface that stubbornly resisted our efforts to remove them.

We are very particular about *Swan*'s appearance, and now she looked like a rust-streaked tramp. She stayed that way until we reached Cape Town, where we learned about oxalic acid. A diluted mixture of this inexpensive acid sloshed on the decks dissolved the rust in a few minutes. The steel particles washed off like grains of sand, leaving the decks bleached snow-white with no adverse effects whatsoever.

The gale blew itself out and a gentle easterly wafted in. As we were preparing to leave, a weather forecast reported another gale headed up out of the Southern Ocean. We retied the mooring lines. The predicted gale blasted through two days later. Was this normal? Why wait for summer if the gales don't abate?

I put this question to a couple of local sailors. They told me that in the winter the busters were more frequent. More frequent! Apparently two or three days of fair weather at a stretch was all one could expect on the tip of this continent.

We finally sailed out of East London, beating south

on the tail end of the gale in an effort to maximize the span of favorable weather that we hoped would follow in its wake. It was imperative that we round Cape Agulhas before the next buster arrived and made it a deadly lee shore. The sailing directions are very explicit in their warnings to Mariners:

> Mariners should remember that off all parts of the south coast of Africa, and especially off salient points, sunken wrecks or uncharted dangers may exist close to the shore; and that it is not advisable to approach this surf-beaten shore, even in full-powered steam-vessels, within a distance of three or four miles; sailing vessels should give Cape Agulhas a berth of seven or eight miles.

A few miles west of Port Elizabeth we crossed back onto the bank. Running before a Force 5 nor'easter, *Swan* bore away across the bight on the run for the cape.

It was on this leg of the passage that we fully appreciated the enormous amount of shipping traffic that marches around the Cape of Good Hope. On one clear night I counted 27 ships during my four-hour watch. Most were oil tankers, eastbound in ballast and westbound laden with Middle East oil.

A large cape is doubled by steering a series of straight courses tangent to the general curve of the coastline. We held one of these courses a few hours too long, which put us to seaward of the desired track and outside most of the tanker traffic. We tacked in toward shore to get away from the edge of the bank and to keep the navigational lights in view. I envisioned a Mr. & Mrs. "Magoo" Moore, sailing through the tankers, completely oblivious to them, while the captains frantically tried to avoid running us down.

With the cape abeam, the wind veered to the southeast, allowing *Swan* to run free. Majestic Table Mountain, the backdrop of the beautiful city of Cape Town, gateway to the Atlantic Ocean, rose with the dawn.

Suddenly I swung the bow away from the land in a northwesterly direction. "If we hold this course for about 60 days, the next thing you'll see will be the Statue of Liberty," I said to the surprised mate. It wasn't a completely whimsical thing. Thoughts of our family and friends at home were on our minds more and more now.

The news of the arrival of our sixth grandchild had reached us in Durban. Molly's two daughters and my two daughters had all married a year or so before we set sail from Portland. In a flurry of fertility they were producing offspring at a rate that made me wonder if we had omitted some critical instruction during the birds-and-the-bees years. This wanton disregard for zero population growth had culminated in a total of eight little people, whom we had never seen, more or less waiting at the dock at the end of our voyage to meet their long-lost grandma and grandpa. Talk about instant geriatrics!

Molly sprang happily into her new role of grandmother while I, being of fragile temperament, sidled reluctantly into the acceptance of the fact that at 45 years of age I was less the daring young adventurer and more the old man of the sea.

As we made fast the lines in a berth at the Royal Cape Yacht Club there was one unhappy note. *Tina* had sailed for St. Helena on the day before our arrival. Vance had left a note for us that read: "The coal dust drove us out. See you somewhere down the road." We were soon to understand what she meant.

Table Mountain creates a venturi effect on the wind, which increases its velocity considerably. The yacht club is to leeward of a busy set of railroad tracks. Not only did the steam locomotives create billowing black smoke, as in East London, but they trundled past pulling long strings of gondolas loaded with coal. The coal dust was driven into every nook and cranny of the boat by the gusting wind, and accumulated against the cockpit coamings like miniature drifts of black snow. We stayed just long enough to complete our provisioning for the Atlantic crossing.

Luderitz, Namibia. We weren't really sure why we were going there, but we were going anyway. It's a lobster-fishing community on the west coast of Africa, 480 miles north of Cape Town. The region has a large concentration of people of German extraction, a legacy of the political maneuvering that took place in Southwest Africa at the close of the 19th Century. A German singlehander had suggested to me in Durban that we go to Luderitz. When I asked him what special attraction Luderitz held that made it worth sailing four or five days along the African coast to get there, he frowned, scratched his chin, reared his head back and said, "Well, I'm going there!" By jing, that was enough for me! "Molly we're going to Luderitz!"

Having sailed 1300 miles along the South African coast, I am convinced that few other places in the world offer such a wide range of unkindly sailing conditions, and the Benguela Current added yet another dimension to the potpourri. This northerly setting current flows along the southwest coast of Africa, bringing frigid water from the Antarctic region and frequently creating heavy fog conditions in a belt extending several miles offshore. I regarded it as the Southern Ocean's last-ditch effort to bring grief to our gallant *Swan*.

We wanted to avoid being caught in the fog and placed in the impotent position of relying on ships sighting us on their radar. For this reason we sailed a course outside the fog belt, 60 miles offshore and parallel to the coastline, in a depth of little more than 100 fathoms.

On the second day out the wind increased in strength, building up steep following seas in the comparatively shallow water, causing *Swan* to pitch and roll in a most uncomfortable way. We were carrying the near-minimum sail—the working jib poled out to starboard. Vane was struggling to hold the course dead downwind. The rogue seas that invariably come roaring along in pairs slued *Swan* this way and that, and at times we were sailing dangerously by the lee. I should have reacted by changing course enough to put the wind on the port quarter, but I didn't, and we paid for my error.

In the wee hours of the morning, when bad things seem prone to happen, BANG! We broached and backwinded the jib.

Molly switched on the spreader lights as we scrambled on deck. We were greeted by the sights and sounds of bedlam on the foredeck. The 14-foot whisker pole had snapped near the center as a result of the tremendous compression load placed on it when the sail backwinded. The section of the pole attached to the mast was hanging down relatively harmless, but the part fastened to the clew of the sail was another matter altogether. As the jib alternately filled and collapsed, the jagged remnant of the pole swung through the air in wild, slashing arcs, delivering crashing blows to the side of the boat.

Swan was wallowing in the trough, lying beam-on to the seas, which was aggravating the situation. I sheeted the jib in as tight as the tangled foreguy would allow. This quieted things considerably and created enough forward drive to regain steerageway. Molly took the helm and steered us off downwind. I made my way forward and found the jib halyard winch by feel, never taking my eyes off that swinging aluminum scimitar for an instant. I released the brake and everything came crashing down on the deck and into the water. The foredeck was covered by a tangle of cables, bridles, and lines that made the Gordian knot look like a slippery hitch.

I was furious with myself for not reacting to the obvious threat of broaching. Maintaining the downwind course in those conditions was a foolish and unnecessary gamble. It flew in the face of the set of rules that had governed my thinking from the outset. It was a cheap lesson, but one that I was having a hard time appreciating while crawling on the rolling, pitching foredeck in the damp chill and half-light, amid the tangle of broken gear.

I lashed the remains of the whisker pole on deck and raised the storm trysail, with which we carried on until daylight.

At sunrise we inspected the side of the boat that had been flogged so violently by the pole—barely a scratch! Miraculously, the pole had hit flat against the side of the boat, and the rub-rail had taken the entire beating.

The wind had diminished to the point that we were moving at a snail's pace under the trysail along. To fly the reacher we had to improvise a substitute for the broken whisker pole. We solved the problem by swinging the main boom out as far as possible, with sufficient elevation to ensure that it wouldn't dip into the sea when the boat rolled. We shackled the boom vang to the toe-rail at a position just forward of the mast, so a strain could be taken downward and forward to counter the mainsheet and topping lift. We then reeved a line from the clew of the sail through a block at the outer end of the boom, back through a block on the toe-rail, and secured it to the forward mooring cleat. This rig served as an adjustable outhaul. The reacher sheet was led to the winch in the normal way. By adjusting the outhaul, the sheets, and the topping lift, we could position the clew of the sail more precisely than when using the actual whisker pole arrangement. We were off and running.

Luderitz lies tucked behind a barren promontory on a well-protected inlet, hidden from the sea. A large cross stands at the top of an imposing craggy monolith which, like a silent sentinel, guards the entrance to the bay. The cross was erected by the Portuguese navigator Bartholomeu Diaz in 1488, during the voyage of exploration on which he discovered the Cape of Good Hope.

If Diaz stopped at that dust bowl in search of water he was wasting his time. For hundreds of miles inland there's nothing but dry sand and rocky hills. Well, hardly anything except diamonds. Thousands of African laborers toil in the diamond mines at a yield ratio of one carat per 300-plus tons of excavated earth. So many, digging so much, for so little.

We motored toward what appeared to be a public dock while gazing at the most unusual town of Luderitz. The architecture was unmistakably Nordic; incongruous in the barren setting. There were no trees or greenery—just sand and rock, like a surrealistic painting of a Bavarian village set in a moonscape.

Suddenly we were aware of several people on the quay waving in our direction. They were so enthusiastic that we glanced behind us, thinking they were waving at someone else. As we came alongside the wharf our welcoming committee helped us tie up against some huge black tires, which are great fenders for ships and great problems for yachts. I later scavenged a wooden plank (no small achievement in the Teutonic orderliness of Luderitz) to use as a buffer against the tires.

Swan was the second American yacht to call at Luderitz in 10 years, and she drew a great deal of attention. A barbecue at the Luderitz Yacht Club was organized on the spot, and began a week-long binge of dinners and parties that nearly wore us out.

The spiny lobster abounds in the local waters, and is the reason Luderitz exists. It is the economic life's blood of the community. We were invited to go along on a Sunday afternoon lobster-trapping excursion. The locals used ring nets, similar to the traps we had used to catch dungeness crabs on the Oregon coast, so we were not complete strangers to their method of trapping those scrappy crustaceans.

The outing was a great success. Our refrigerator and freezer were overflowing with lobster. We stuffed ourselves so outrageously with this delicious and rich delicacy that by week's end the mere thought of lobster tail in drawn butter was enough to turn off our appetites completely.

A local shipwright shaped a piece of "Oregon" to insert as a splint in the broken whisker pole. South Africans, New Zealanders, and Australians tend to categorize all lumber imported from the northwestern part of the United States and Canada as "Oregon." They make no distinction between fir, hemlock, pine, or spruce, and no amount of arguing will change their minds. I had given up on the subject after an incident in Sydney. An Australian fellow was admiring *Swan*'s boom. "Nice quality Oregon," he said. "Fine grain."

"Well actually it's spruce," I said.

"Sorry mate, I know a piece of Oregon when I see it," he stated categorically.

Without raising my voice, which required a supreme effort, I said, "It's just that I built this boat; I purchased the timber. I knew that boom when it was a spruce log."

Then, taking him gently by the arm, I led him around to the stern of the boat. There, beneath the name *Swan*, were the words *Portland, Oregon*

"That's where I'm from," I said. "O-R-E-G-O-N."

"That's right mate, that's where Oregon comes from," he said, and he hurried off down the dock.

I thanked the old craftsman for the fine job of shaping the "Oregon" and toted it back to the boat, where Molly was attending to the last-minute details of preparation for a long ocean passage. There were no diversions left. It was waiting, unchanged for millenniums— the South Atlantic Ocean. It was time to venture forth into that vast body of water that, when crossed, would put us in our own backyard. We did, on a Sunday afternoon.

12

*B*RAZIL. IT has an exotic ring to it. It brings to mind the bolero, the flamenco. One can see svelte dancing girls in flaming red dresses, bright-colored flowers in their jet-black hair, twirling under the stars to the strains of guitars; castanets held high, clicking to the beat of the music while the soft, caressing breeze carries with it the sounds of laughter and ice tinkling in a glass.

I snapped back to reality, and the reality was fog—thick, dank, all-embracing fog. It rolled in just after sunset on the last breath of a moribund southerly and closed around us like a shroud. Fog in daylight at sea is bad enough; it's a nightmare after dark. Our world shrank to an irreducible hemisphere of blackness. We were 35 miles offshore, rolling in the swell without the slightest trace of a breeze. For a short time we motored, but we stopped because the engine noise eliminated any chance of hearing a ship. Plowing blindly through the fog "damning the torpedoes" produced an anxiety that my nervous system could not begin to tolerate.

It was dead quiet. I stared unseeing into the murky gloom. It was easy to imagine a frothy white bow wave being pushed at 15 knots by a towering wall of steel, bursting upon us from out of the blackness. I looked up apprehensively to where I reckoned the radar reflector was hanging. I hoped it was busily bouncing sharp signals at the speed of light back to the glowing radar screens on the bridges of the charging monsters. I wasn't even sure that the reflector worked.

There was nothing more to do on deck. I went below, where the mate was preparing dinner—lobster again! I'd been all set for hamburgers and beer, and had a strong notion to tell her about the wall of steel and frothy bow wave.

I took the first watch, which was an exercise in futility under the circumstances. Molly switched off the light and went to sleep as if she were living in Suburbia, U.S.A.

I studied the Atlantic chart. The big blank space between Africa and South America looked even larger in the dim red glow of the chart light. It was difficult to imagine crossing that great expanse of water in anything slower than a Boeing 747. Near the center of the blank space was a small dot of land, the island of St. Helena, Napoleon's place of exile. It was our next intended landfall, 1300 miles to the west. Then it was on to Natal, Brazil, where the tinkling ice and dancing girls were waiting, 1800 miles west of St. Helena. All we needed was a little wind. The night dragged on.

At 0200 I gave up the pointless watch and fell asleep in the dampness of the cockpit.

Shortly after what appeared to be dawn, our minia-ture world changed from black to gray, and with sunrise a zephyr stole in from the southwest. The reacher and mainsail began to flutter gently and fill. Within the hour the fog had completely cleared and we were reaching smartly on the port tack, bathed in glorious sunshine.

The color of the sea had changed from murky gray to a deepwater blue. Slick brown bewhiskered seals peered curiously at us with their countenances of per-petual surprise as *Swan* cut through the smooth, cold seas, making six knots, west by northwest. The world was right again.

On the fifth day of the passage we crossed the Straits of Gibraltar-to-Cape of Good Hope shipping track. Molly took the first night watch and I cautioned her to be especially alert for traffic from the north and south.

From a deep sleep I heard the now-familiar "Jimmy, I see a light." Thousands of miles of blue water had passed beneath *Swan*'s keel since those early days when the mate's call from the cockpit would bring me on deck in a state of alarm. She had become a first-rate watchkeeper and I had complete confidence that the ship was as safe on her watch as on mine. It was standard procedure that she awaken me if there were reason to believe that we were sailing into harm's way, and that was exactly what *Swan* was doing on this clear, crisp, South Atlantic night.

A ship was approaching from the north. Its port running light was intermittently visible, and the range lights were open a few degrees, indicating that we were a point or two on her port bow. We watched the distance between us close for a quarter of an hour without any noticeable change in the relative bearing of the ship. It was becoming increasingly apparent that *Swan* and a large ship were bent on occupying the same spot in the ocean at the same time.

I attempted to contact the ship by VHF radio without success. *Swan* was lit up like a Christmas tree, easily visible on this clear night. Apparently the lookout hadn't seen us, or if he had, the fact of our existence wasn't influencing the course and speed of his ship.

In less than a minute the reacher was taken in and the engine started. I shifted into reverse and stopped all forward motion to let the blind behemoth pass in front of us. Then, when the ship was less than a quarter of a mile away it made a panic turn to port, heeling sharply as it did. For a few horrifying seconds we were dead in her path, looking down the barrel at aligned range lights and both red and green lanterns. I jammed the gearshift into forward and gave the engine full throttle. *Swan* ran for her life! I shall never forget the sight of that ship and the sound of her throbbing engines as she steamed past close on our stern, with her great hulk silhouetted against the night sky.

The mate raised the sail and I went below. I lay shaken in the bunk, wondering how it's possible for a singlehanded sailor to sleep with no one on watch.

On the afternoon of February 12, 1980 at 19°20'S, we crossed the Prime Meridian, returning to the western hemisphere that we had sailed out of nearly two years before. Since leaving Portland *Swan* had traversed 238 degrees of longitude and sailed 20,000 nautical miles. Now she was running westward with a bone in her teeth.

The trades never faltered, ranging from Force 3 to 5 and blowing in the general direction of our course. We had learned the hard way about running dead downwind, although Vane could have easily handled it in these conditions. We played it safe by sailing a course 10 degrees high, putting the wind on the quarter. We held this point of sail for two days, whereupon we jibed to the opposite tack. Every other day we obliquely crossed the rhumbline, and very little distance was lost.

St. Helena loomed up fine on the port bow with the dawning of the thirteenth day of this leisurely passage. The tops of the bluish-gray mountains were cloaked in fluffy white clouds, and as we drew nearer we could see giant, curling combers thundering against the base of the sheer cliffs on the windward shore. We sailed into the lee of a prominent headland and ghosted toward the anchorage at Jamestown.

The anchorage leaves a lot to be desired. There's a constant swell in the cove that culminates in breakers that crash with tremendous force against an earth-backed seawall fronting the town. The thundering roar was so intimidating that for a time we considered not stopping at all. But the threat was more in our minds than in reality, as the prevailing breeze was offshore and it would require a major shift in the tradewinds to make the situation dangerous.

Still, it was worrisome. I put out a more-than-ample 250 feet of chain in 30 feet of water and dove to check the set of the anchor. In open roadsteads or any anchorage perceived as potentially hazardous, it is very reassuring to see the anchor buried in sand with the end of the shank barely protruding and the heavy chain running along the bottom, then rising upward toward the boat in a shock-absorbing catenary curve. With *Swan*'s engine in full reverse the last 100 feet of chain never lifted from the bottom.

Landing the dinghy at the quay required the close-quarter seamanship of a Newfoundland doryman, the reflexes of a mongoose, and a fair degree of reckless abandon—the last of the three being the only requirement we felt we could fill.

There was a line hanging down from an overhead support at a landing place on the quay to facilitate the often-abortive attempts at dinghy docking. The surging swell was there, but the seas didn't break at that particular spot. An attempted landing anywhere else along the quay would have resulted in the dinghy and probably its occupants being reduced to bits and pieces.

In preparation for our assault on the landing place we triple-wrapped the camera in plastic bags, blowing air into the outer one so the camera would float if disaster struck. I told Molly to protect the camera if we were knocked against the seawall, as she would heal and the camera wouldn't. This remark, however, was not received in the jocular spirit in which it was uttered.

Not a lot happens at St. Helena in the way of

entertainment, and a group of islanders had gathered on the quay to watch our performance at the landing—like Romans watching a contest between Christians and lions. "Wait for a lull, wait for a lull in the swell," one of the men shouted to us.

A lull is when the rise and fall of the water at the platform is five feet instead of seven. At the next "lull" I backed the dinghy against the seawall, and as the water rose, Molly swung smartly ashore like Jane from the jungle. I quickly handed her the camera just before the elevator went to the basement. On the next surge I swung ashore, pulling the dinghy after me with a poetry of motion that would have scored at least a 9.9 by an unbiased panel of judges. Some of the bystanders nodded their approval, though somewhat disappointedly, it seemed to me.

Picturesque Jamestown lies in a valley that rises sharply from the sea into flax-covered mountains. It is the main settlement on the 47-square-mile island, and there are a few other small communities scattered about on the mountain slopes.

St. Helena has had a very turbulent history for such an isolated place, but its isolation has been the principal reason for the turbulence. In the 19th Century the island lay in the path of clipper ships that plied the trade between the western world and the Far East. Large shipping firms such as the British East India Company used St. Helena as a fresh food and water depot for ships employed in the trade. As many as 1500 ships called there each year—an incredible average of four ships arriving and leaving that remote speck in the ocean every day of the year.

The island was discovered by the Portuguese in 1502. It was promptly taken from them by force by the Dutch, who lost it in the same manner to the British in 1658. England's sea power ensured British dominion of the island thereafter, and in 1834 St. Helena officially became a British possession.

In 1815 St. Helena's most famous resident, Napoleon, was exiled by the British to the island, where he lived until his death in 1821. He wasn't exactly alone. His entourage numbered no less than 50 people, and they were guarded by 3000 British troops, which would seem more than adequate to guard a fellow five feet, four inches in height.

The British were so worried about the security of their slippery prisoner that they built a fortress spanning the entire seaboard in front of Jamestown, complete with a moat and a massive parapet with crenels, through which cannons guarded the seaward approaches. It is still intact, and the government offices are presently located within its walls.

It all appeared somewhat redundant to us when we considered that an invading force would eventually have to contend with that bone-crushing seawall.

Napoleon's home is situated high on a mountain overlooking a lush green valley. We hired an islander to drive us there. Molly and I were the only visitors that day, and we received a guided tour of the French general's last residence by an old fellow who clearly enjoyed talking about the history of the place.

We could almost see and hear Napoleon and his aides in animated conversation around the huge, polished diningroom table; reliving campaigns, the great victories and defeats, with glasses being filled with vintage wine.

So completely was I caught up in the historical atmosphere and by a full-sized portrait of Napoleon that I nearly knocked myself senseless on one of the sawed-off emperor's five-foot, nine-inch doorways.

It was time to move on. One complete day was spent washing clothes and filling the water tanks. This was accomplished in several trips via the infamous landing. Through overconfidence born of my earlier performance, I bungled a docking approach and was thrown into the water, losing an excellent pair of sunglasses and my cockiness in one fell swoop.

The sun was setting as we raised the anchor and took our departure from St. Helena, that tranquil island outpost standing strangely alone in a great sea. With her wings spread, *Swan* filled away to the west.

13

OUR LASTING impression of the South Atlantic is of a boring stretch of salt water, devoid of characteristics that set one body of water apart from another, like the deviousness of the Tasman Sea, or the Indian Ocean's large rolling swells and teeming sealife. During the entire passage we saw not one seabird, and the trolling lines were out day and night for 1100 miles without a strike.

Day after day *Swan* plugged along in the gentle trades flying only the reacher. We rigged a cockpit awning and spent many hours reading and writing in the shade it provided. All the ports and hatches were open and it was almost as if we were lying at anchor, yet each succeeding day would find us 110 miles or so down the track. We weren't complaining.

In the middle of the night on March 4, 1980, in the vicinity of 8°S, 27°W, something happened that dramatically dispelled the comfortable boredom. The moon was hidden by heavy cloud cover on this balmy tropical night. I had just made a course correction on the steering vane and was squinting to read the compass when the night became day. For a fearful moment I thought we were in the beam of a powerful searchlight, but there wasn't a ship to be seen, and I could see the horizon in all directions as if it were high noon. Bathed in the bright light I ranged between outright panic and doubting my sanity. Then I discovered the source—a brilliant, bluish-white light such as an arc lamp creates was descending through the clouds with orange fire trailing behind. I stared dumbfounded, trying to fathom what was happening. This wasn't a meteor. Was it a UFO? It seemed almost supernatural. Surely it wasn't ... no, that's impossible—of all the places on the earth this just couldn't be the site of the Second Coming! But the Good Book said it would be unexpected, and Lord knows that prerequisite had been met to the nines.

Just as I was preparing myself for the awesome responsibility of being mankind's unworthy committee of one to welcome the descending Deity (the mate could sleep through a nuclear war), the white light burned out. Smoldering debris fell into the water, and I was once again cloaked in darkness—darkness intensified by the total destruction of my night vision. I sat in the corner of the cockpit trying to decide if it had really happened.

A Voice of America newscast later that day provided a more mundane explanation: A man-made satellite had reentered the atmosphere and fallen into the sea in our area. Skylab had missed us by a thousand miles, but NASA was finding the range!

On the evening of the fifteenth day of the passage the loom of the city lights of Natal appeared faintly on the horizon. The next day was a Saturday, and at 0700 we crossed the Potengi River bar, Porto de Natal, weaving our way through the multifarious fishing fleet that was headed out to sea under sail.

Thus far in the voyage we had never experienced serious language difficulties. English is so widely spoken that communication had never been a problem—until Natal. They speak Portuguese, and by and large no English. English is our only language.

The first round of a week-long bout that we steadily lost began at the Porto de Natal Yacht Club, an enigmatic place that didn't seem to have any members. We picked a spot to moor behind another yacht tied along a stone pier in front of the club.

A wiry, wrinkled old man arrived at the pier to direct us. He was, as we were to find out later, perpetually intoxicated, and acted as a self-appointed dockmaster. His bloodshot eyes were partially covered by eyelids at half-mast, and he wore a hand-sewn blue denim beanie that added a final touch to his strange appearance. He, like the English in India during the past century, believed that anyone can be made to understand a foreign language if the words are bellowed loudly enough.

The upshot of this distracting encounter was that we failed to check the depth of the water. Suddenly I noticed that the deck felt too steady—like sitting-on-the-bottom steady! The tide was ebbing, fast. I slammed the engine into reverse and backed down hard. We never moved an inch. We didn't have time to launch the dinghy, so we broke out the stern anchor, tied it to an empty jerry can with a slippery hitch, and threw it over the side. I jumped into the water and swam the buoyed anchor offshore while Molly payed out the line. I released the slipknot, let the anchor go, and swam back. Molly put the engine in full reverse while I heaved on the kedge anchor with the aid of a sheet winch. Not a chance. Not for the next 12 hours anyway.

The tide was moving out smartly now, and to make matters worse we were beginning to heel toward the ugly stone pier. Again I was over the side, swimming against the ebbing tide toward a mooring buoy about 50 feet from the boat, towing a line that was tied around my waist. With burning lungs and muscles, I reached the slimy, barnacle-encrusted buoy, fastened the line to it, and clung there exhausted. It suddenly occurred to me there might be leeches, poisonous snakes, or even crocodiles in this murky river. We were, after all, in the equatorial belt in South America. With a regenerated spirit that would befit an Olympic gold medalist, I churned out the distance separating *Swan* and me, doing the Amazon freestyle.

Using the jib halyard to gain leverage from the masthead, we took a strain on the line that was attached to the buoy. Slowly *Swan* heeled away from the jagged rocks of the pier. That began her ignominious starboard descent to ground zero, center stage, flags all standing.

It was then that I took a closer look at the 30-foot sloop moored ahead of us. She was the Judas goat that had lured us into shallow water in the first place. There she stood, securely tied to a piling, ready to have her bottom scrubbed at low tide. I stood on the rapidly heeling deck, furious at my carelessness, while a few feet away Halfmast bawled and bellowed at me in slurred Portuguese.

The harbormaster had informed us by radio that the customs and immigration authorities would be with us straightaway. That had been four hours earlier. *Swan* was now lying on the sand, high and dry, like a beached whale. A small crowd had gathered on the shore, watching the spectacle. Molly picked off a gooseneck barnacle here, a bit of eelgrass there, while I made some close examinations of the propeller and underwater fittings— two savvy gringos who had careened their yacht for inspection right in front of the yacht club. It wasn't necessary to understand Portuguese to know that our gallery wasn't buying our act for a minute.

Into this ludicrous scene came Inspector Roberto Salazar, Departmento de Policia Federal. He stood on the pier, motioning in an imperious manner for me to come ashore. I waded through the tidepools with our passports and ship's papers, and introduced myself. The inspector flipped out his wallet containing his official identification with such an exaggerated flourish that I almost laughed in his face. He then said, "Meester Moore, I am like the FBI in your country."

"Very well," I said, "what can I do for you, sir?"

"Passports and visas," he barked, holding out his hand.

Taken aback by the tone of his voice, I handed him our passports and explained that from information contained in our government-issued traveler's information booklet, it was my understanding that a United States citizen was not required to have a visa for a visit to Brazil for 30 days or less, and that we didn't have them.

"That is all changed," he said sharply. "Your country now chooses to make Brazilian people have visas to visit the United States; therefore, you must have a visa to visit Brazil. You don't have a visa. You must leave—now!"

It was all becoming clear to me. President Carter's human rights policies were having a backlash. Great! Make half of Latin America angry and then give up jurisdiction over the Panama Canal. Stumbling along, ill-informed, on the cutting edge of U.S. foreign policy wasn't part of our cruising plans. *Swan* and crew could get into real trouble.

"Leave now! How can we leave now when the ocean's gone?" I asked, pointing toward *Swan*. Then, calming myself, I said, "Senor Salazar, we've just come in from two weeks at sea and we need a day or two of rest."

"That is most unfortunate, Meester Moore, but you must leave when your boat floats again. While you are waiting you may take on water," he said, smiling broadly. Roberto was all heart.

Suddenly I remembered something from the maritime law education I received from an old merchant sailor in the hallowed halls of Monty's Tavern in Beaverton, Oregon: Under international maritime law, a vessel that is in need of repair, the neglect of which would place ship and crew in jeopardy, is allowed a minimum of 24 hours (by the adherent countries) to effect the necessary repairs.

A small welding job that we had been putting off until we reached Florida suddenly blossomed into a matter of life or death. Looking Roberto straight in the eye, I said, "It isn't only rest we need, sir. We need to have some critical welding done."

The Inspector was something of a locker-room lawyer himself, and immediately replied, "If your ship is not seaworthy you have 24 hours to correct the problem."

"Where can we have the welding done on the weekend?" I asked, sounding as earnest as I possibly could.

After a thoughtful silence Roberto said, "There is no welding done on the weekend. You will have to leave on Monday."

"But Senor Salazar, if our 24 hours begins on Monday morning, wouldn't our time for leaving be Tuesday morning?" I felt more like Clarence Darrow with each passing minute.

A long silence followed. Roberto's eyes flicked from one side to the other. "I suppose that is correct Meester Moore, but you *must* leave on Tuesday."

Roberto handed me our passports and instructed me to report to the police station on Monday to apprise them of our progress with the repairs. I thanked him and assured him that we would report to the station before noon on Monday without fail.

It had been dark for two hours when we finally floated free of the bottom, moved into deeper water, and anchored. There were no svelte dancing girls, but in their place was a host of flies and mosquitoes. We went below, tired, hot, angry, and hungry. I poured us two large belts of whiskey.

On Monday morning our earthshaking welding job

was handled by a skilled welder who was doing some repair work on an American offshore oil rig tender. We then set off to report to the police station—prior to noon, as agreed.

Two officers at the police station examined our documents, even though it was obvious that they could not read English. With sign language and the assistance of a passerby who spoke some English, we were able to make them understand that our boat had been repaired and that we would remain eternally grateful for the gracious hospitality extended to us. I tried to get them to stamp or sign one of the many documents that had been issued to us to show that we had complied with Roberto's instructions. This request was met by blank stares and shrugs. We went back to the boat.

Molly and I were both feeling ill from the effects of a shrimp dinner we had eaten the night before at what was supposed to be a first-class restaurant. We were resting on board *Swan* in the afternoon, grateful for the breeze that wafted down the forward hatch; grateful for the screens that kept the swarms of insects at bay, and grateful that we would soon be leaving.

All of this gratefulness was shattered by coarse shouting from the pier. Two uniformed men who looked like fugitives from a Mission Impossible set motioned me ashore. I rowed to the pier, where I was confronted by these seedy characters. They gruffly sent me back to the boat to get Molly and our papers. I was beginning to feel uneasy.

As we both came ashore one of the men, a simpleton who talked with a cigarette dangling from his lips, jerked our passports from Molly's hand. This engendered such a sharp response from the mate that it surprised me and startled the uniformed bully. It infuriated me to see this jackass representative of a regime that didn't recognize basic freedoms manhandling our United States passports. The plight of the American hostages in Iran crossed my mind.

Without explanation we were spirited away in the back seat of an automobile through the streets of Natal. Thoroughly bewildered, and more than a little worried, we were led into a government office complex. People were seated on benches along the walls; people inured to waiting with hat in hand for some bureaucrat to grant them some "privilege" that in America would be an automatic right of citizenship.

Into the room came Roberto, his imperious manner fully intact. In his presence the simpleton with the cigarette underwent a change from swaggering bully to a bowing and scraping sycophant. Molly put her hand lightly on my arm, cautioning restraint. It wasn't necessary though—Clarence Darrow was rapidly losing his glibness.

"Meester Moore, why did you not report to the police as I instructed you to do?"

I stood up to my full six feet two inch height so the little prima donna would have to look up at me in front of those self-effacing, browbeaten people in the waiting room.

"Senor Salazar, we were at the police station before noon today and spent considerable time there," I said, and I gave him the station's address.

In a shrill voice he said, "That is the local police station! I meant here, the Departmento de Policia Federal!" He was barely able to restrain himself from stamping his foot.

This cat-and-mouse game was making me more nervous by the minute. I apologized for my error while Roberto listened impassively.

They proceeded to take mug shots of us, and fingerprinted all of our fingers, both thumbs, and palms. To the consternation of the photographer, and me, Molly took a hairbrush from her purse and brushed her hair before having her mug shots taken.

By this time my imagination was in orbit. I visualized myself in chains, languishing in a rat-infested dungeon in tattered rags and unkempt beard, taping messages to Molly through thick stone walls while Roberto entertained guests on gala afternoon sails on *Swan*, swilling down our last few bottles of South African wine. At least the United States government knew of the existence of the hostages in Iran. Not a soul outside of Natal had the vaguest idea where we were. I thereupon reiterated my apologies with such phony contrition that I couldn't stand myself for days afterward.

After a few admonitions about how one conducts oneself while visiting Brazil, and how the regime was completely misunderstood by the rest of the world, Roberto then turned on the charm, wishing us a pleasant voyage and other niceties. I felt so nauseated from the bad seafood, the stress, and the stifling heat, that it took every bit of self-control I could muster to keep from vomiting on the floor at the end of Roberto's little speech. I am reasonably certain that would have pushed him over the brink.

We hastily brought water on board, along with a large bag of avocados that sold for three cents each. This was the sum total of our provisioning at Natal. We both had diarrhea, and I was vomiting on a regular basis, but it didn't matter a whit—we were leaving. The risk of perishing at sea from some insidious disease was far easier to abide than the thought of spending another hour in Brazil. It was, however, not to be.

It wasn't only the spirit of Murphy's Law we were experiencing, but the exact letter of it: The anchor had fouled on a submerged mooring cable. For the first time in many months we hadn't rigged a trip line when the bottom wasn't visible. It was hopelessly fouled.

I knelt on the bow and gazed woozily at the anchor chain leading down into the murky depths. The scenario ran wild through my fuzzy brain: After procrastinating for a while I would summon my courage and dive into the murky depths. I would become entangled in some awful submerged trap and Molly would be widowed on the spot, a defenseless girl at the mercy of the tyrant Roberto.

Just as I was preparing myself for the 20-foot dive, two teenage boys straddling a large plank paddled out to the boat. They had perceived the problem and had come out to assist us. I gave them diving masks and they made a reconnoitering dive. On the second dive, a long one, they surfaced and gave us the thumbs up sign. We were free! At the risk of being regarded as an Ugly American, I handed a fistful of cruzeiros to these two brown-skinned angels. Happily, our last memory of Brazil was of two boys sitting astride a floating timber, with big smiles on their faces, waving goodbye.

We managed to hank on the working jib and set the vane to steer us on a course perpendicular to the coastline to put distance between *Swan* and Brazil as quickly as possible. Sick and retching, we sailed over the bar and into the clean, grand, free, blue Atlantic.

14

THERE ARE basically two routes to St. Petersburg, Florida from the eastern approaches of the Caribbean. One has the option of sailing south of Cuba through the Yucatan Channel, or north of the island through the reef-lined Old Bahama Channel. The Yucatan Channel is wide, and the northerly setting current is favorable. The Old Bahama Channel is narrow, with less favorable currents, and forces yachts to sail for many miles within sight of Cuba. We were wary of taking unnecessary risks after our experience in Brazil, and we had no way of knowing what might have transpired between Jimmy and Fidel. We chose the southern route.

There was another reason that influenced this decision: We had invited my uncle, who lives in St. Petersburg, to make a passage with us, and Grand Cayman, a small, pro-everybody island located 160 miles south of Cuba was a good spot to meet him.

My uncle, Glen Gallagher, was a special uncle from the start. As children, my brothers and I looked forward with great anticipation to his visits. We found it almost unbearable that he had fallen into the bad habit of most adults, in those days before television, of spending far too much time engaged in grown-up conversation, while tucked away in his pocket, or his mind, his latest magic trick lay captive. How we dreaded any question my father might ask him that would prolong this gross waste of time. Surely my dad knew that in the other room, inside a black leather case, was my uncle's movie projector with his latest home movie, and most likely a *Felix The Cat* reel, and, without fail, the runaway buzz-saw cartoon, which in the discerning minds of the Moore brothers would have easily eclipsed *Gone With the Wind* for pure undiluted entertainment. I welcomed the opportunity to entertain him for a change.

The equatorial currents that flow westward along the northern coast of South America eventually coalesce into the Gulf Stream. Tobago, a small island in the southern part of the Caribbean, lies in the heart of this powerful flow of water. It was our next port of call, and the 1850-mile, current-assisted passage was completed in 12 days, 16 hours; an average of 146 miles per day.

A Force 4 to 5 nor'easter blew steadily. We poled the reacher out to port, where it stayed untouched for the entire passage. We felt as if we were somehow cheating, to be moving along so swiftly while expending so little effort. But we had only to recall the grueling days spent thrashing to windward in the Tasman Sea and the Southern Ocean, bone weary, fighting for every mile against fierce gales, to banish such foolish thoughts.

On March 19, 1980 we crossed the equator, and a few days later Polaris peeked over the horizon for the first time in two years.

The current was like a river. Near 10°N we were becalmed for eight hours. We took star-sights in the morning and, to ascertain the speed of the current, an observation of the sun and upper limb of the moon at noon. During the seven hours that had elapsed between fixes we had moved 21 miles westward toward Tobago with the sails down, dead in the water, at three knots, with the bow of the boat pointed south toward Surinam!

Morning and evening star-fixes were the order of the day until Tobago hove into view, sharply silhouetted against a cobalt-blue sky.

In the town of Scarborough we wandered along the commercial wharf looking for anyone who could direct us to the Port Captain's office. Molly approached a young man standing at the gangway of a small coaster, *Bluewing*, out of Parimaribo, Surinam. The fellow could not speak English, so he invited us on board to talk with the captain.

The captain, a white-haired black man who wore tiny Benjamin Franklin-style glasses low on his nose, ambled across the deck toward us and with an engaging smile shook our hands. "I'm Captain Marville."

Molly and I looked at each other for an instant as we tried to squelch the humorous vision of the good captain dressed in a skintight lavender suit, springing from the bridge deck, crimson cape trailing, bent on apprehending Tobago's wrongdoers. He then thoroughly surprised us in very precise English, spoken in that lilting Caribbean manner, with a twinkle in his eye: "I imagine that you have never met a comic strip character before."

He invited us to his quarters for cocktails, as the sun was over the yardarm. (*Bluewing* was equipped with an adjustable yardarm.) The amiable captain placed his ship at our disposal for the duration of our stay at Scarborough. A real laundry room and hot showers!

An American yacht with two fellows on board arrived at the anchorage late one night. They had sailed from Tenerife in the Canary Islands, bound for Barbados, which they "narrowly missed" by 380 miles. They had more or less run into Guyana, South America, discovering where they were by employing a simple navigational expedient: They had asked a local fisherman what country they had reached.

The skipper had planned to reacquaint himself with the essentials of navigation during the voyage; a plan that worked more successfully in theory at the dock in Tenerife than in the lonely expanse of the Atlantic

Ocean. Both of these cheerful fellows had lost a considerable amount of weight.

We invited them to dinner on board *Swan* one evening. In view of their undernourished condition, Molly prepared a large quantity of food, which turned out to be barely enough. Huge mounds of spaghetti had disappeared from their plates before I had finished my salad. After dinner I broke out the brandy and we talked far into the night.

Their immediate plan was to sail directly to their original destination, Barbados, which lay 130 miles to the north-northeast. This would put their old wooden ketch hard on the wind, beating against the vigorous Northeast Trades and fighting a westward-setting current flowing at nearly three knots. I suggested that they attempt something that had a better chance of success, like sailing up Niagara Falls.

On the following day, at the skipper's request, I gave him a refresher course in celestial navigation. He had been omitting the critical sight-reduction step of calculating the local hour angle of the celestial body. This could be compared to assembling an internal combustion engine without installing the pistons.

Several months later, in Florida, we received a letter from the skipper. They had island-hopped their way through the Lesser Antilles and, risking the wrath of Fidel, made the passage to the east coast of the United States via the Old Bahama Channel. We have a special feeling for those two seat-of-the-pants sailors.

Not only do mad dogs and Englishmen, but also cruising sailors go out in the noonday sun. To add a bit of challenge, they lug jerry cans full of fuel down hot dusty roads; they struggle with them over slippery rocks and seawalls; they sweat like mules; they wade through the surf and clamber aboard dinghies and lay to the oars with a will on the long row to the anchorage until, at last, the tanks are topped off. A cooling plunge over the side, and the refueling is over for another couple of months. It's not always that primitive, but it was like that at Scarborough.

Pedro Banks had me worried. It is an unlit shoal area 30 miles south of Jamaica, with a bewildering current running through its scattered rocks and reefs. The rhumbline to Grand Cayman passed between Jamaica and the banks. I was more on edge with each passing hour as we approached the point, east of the island, where the decision had to be made to stay the course and risk the hazards of the banks, or turn north, taking the longer but safer route through the channel separating Jamaica and Cuba. The northern route wouldn't be easy. *Swan* would be hard on the wind sweeping down through the Windward Passage.

At this stage of the voyage we had ample precedent to assist us in making the correct decision when comfort and a fast passage were being weighed against risk. We personally knew of two yachts that now lay at the bottom of the sea because their skippers opted for comfort when faced with a similar decision. We hardened the sheets and hauled to the north with no way of knowing that this seemingly prudent choice would place us in peril of another kind.

In the early afternoon the Northeast Trades began to increase in force. Whitecapped seas were forming, promising a rough slog through the channel. Molly and I were on deck tucking a second reef in the mainsail when we became aware of the distant drone of an engine. Scanning the horizon we saw a small powerboat closing with us from the southwest. We quickly completed our work on deck and returned to the cockpit, where we watched with a growing uneasiness as the boat drew nearer.

We, like nearly everyone involved in boating, have on many occasions waved a friendly greeting to fellow boaters and enjoyed the camaraderie of it all. Why then should this approaching boat cause us anxiety? Our complete isolation was, of course, the reason. There was no familiar landmark just ahead, no crowded anchorage a mile or two away. Our lonely world was comprised of about 30 square miles, empty except for us and this powerboat, coming directly at us for no apparent reason. It commanded our undivided attention.

Warnings issued by the United States Coast Guard were explicit about the danger of yacht hijackings in the Caribbean, and counseled extreme caution. Many boats had disappeared under mysterious circumstances in those waters in recent years. A blood- and bullet-spattered derelict yacht had just been found a few days earlier, drifting off the Florida Keys with its crew unaccounted for.

It soon became absolutely clear that the approaching boat was on a course that would intercept us. Prudence dictated that we assume the worst and hope we were wrong. I sent Molly below to get the rifle and also to get her out of sight. The people on board the oncoming boat could only guess at the size of *Swan*'s crew. It was important that they not learn how vulnerable we actually were.

I felt a rush of fear course through me. Who were they? Why were they coming toward us? It didn't appear to be a fishing boat. I could think of no legitimate reason why they would be pursuing us, and I was certain no good would come of it if they were allowed to come near.

Molly appeared at the companionway, ashen-faced, with the loaded rifle in one hand and a box of ammunition in the other. Suddenly my fear was supplanted by anger. We were sailing along, not violating any laws, and now these interlopers had us running scared. I resolved that *Swan* and crew would not be an easy mark. They would board our boat literally over my dead body.

When the pursuing boat was about 600 yards off our port quarter I started the engine and applied full power forward. From a crouching position I closehauled the jib and mainsail. A quick adjustment of the steering vane and *Swan* came up hard on the wind. I reasoned that while it would be rough for us, it would be rougher still for them. This was soon proven to be true. Our pursuers would rise on the crest of a sea and then plunge into the trough. If they had weapons, the possibility of using them with any degree of accuracy was greatly diminished.

There appeared to be three men on board. However, there were elements in the situation that helped neutralize their advantage: I had become proficient at holding the scope of a sextant steady on the horizon from a rolling, pitching boat, and aiming a rifle is about the same. In a shoot-out I would be firing from a more stable platform. I was never exposed, while they were clearly visible each time they rode down the face of a sea. I didn't have to steer. And I am a very good shot with a rifle.

The increased pounding impeded their progress, but the distance between us was slowly closing. One of the men stood up and began hacking at his wrist with his other hand, signaling us to cut our engines, to stop. I emphatically waved them away while keenly watching for any show of weapons. They disregarded my gestures to bear off. Molly handed me the rifle.

About 60 yards separated us. The general appearance of the men did nothing to allay my fear, which was rapidly eroding away my anger and righteous indignation.

I had formed a sketchy plan from the jumble of thoughts racing through my mind. If a show of the rifle didn't cause them to hesitate, I would fire a warning shot above their heads. Should they continue the pursuit in the face of the warning, my next shot would be aimed at the heart of the man driving the boat. If it came to that, the shooting wasn't going to stop when the driver went down.

With my heart beating like a trip-hammer I raised the rifle to my shoulder in a way that exhibited its profile, lest our pursuers mistake it for something else. Then I aimed it squarely at the man who was still moronically hacking his wrist.

Never before had I seen such a look of complete surprise as the wide-eyed, gaping expression on the face of the man staring into the muzzle of the rifle. To my great and everlasting relief, implementing my contingency plan wasn't necessary. The show of the weapon was enough. They throttled down sharply, nearly broaching in the process.

I adjusted the steering vane to a close reach to increase our speed. Through binoculars we observed our erstwhile companions, who were engaged in animated conversation. With what seemed to be great reluctance, they turned away to the south.

My knees were like jelly. I slumped down against the cabin. Our worst moments at sea, when nature's forces were the most ferocious, had not frightened us anywhere near as much as three of our fellow humans just had. The forces of nature are formidable, but they are not evil.

We spent a lot of time rehashing this frightening experience. Were they indeed pirates? Could we have handled the situation differently? I don't know the answer to those questions, but I do know that we are still alive to tell the tale.

One incontrovertible fact emerged from the incident. The threat created by the rifle, and that alone, deterred our pursuers. Only one time during the four-year voyage was it necessary to defend ourselves. Fortunately we had the means to do so.

North of Jamaica the wind diminished to the point

that *Swan* crept through the channel at a snail's pace. Off Montego Bay I repeatedly played "Jamaica Farewell" on the ukulele, to no avail. The island was in view for three days, and then the wind came as suddenly as it had died.

The Cayman Islanders have a history of luring visitors to their shores. Today's enticements are beautiful beaches and tax shelters; in bygone days, according to legend, they would lead a horse carrying a ship's lantern along the surf-beaten windward shore in hopes that the captain of a passing ship would be duped into believing it was another ship, and that his own vessel had strayed off course. If he were deceived by this ruse and changed course to pass closer to the island, there was a good chance that his ship would be wrecked on the reef. The scoundrels responsible for the deception would then salvage the booty.

Rusting away on this rugged shore lie the hulks of two freighters. The abrupt end to their maritime service was not the result of treachery. Most likely they were driven on the rocks by one of the violent hurricanes that sweep through the Caribbean every year. They did, however, add a certain flavor to the legend.

My uncle flew to Grand Cayman in a reasonably comfortable jet airplane at about 500 knots in order to sail back to Florida in a marginally comfortable sailing yacht at about five knots. It sort of made me wonder. I never asked him why he would do such a thing, because I was afraid that he might pose a similar question to me.

Sailing wasn't something new to Glen. He'd learned to sail down in Trinidad in 1938, when war clouds were gathering and Molly and I were just two years old. In later years he sailed on Wolf Lake in northern Indiana, where I was born and raised. As a boy, I had it on good authority from an older buddy who was almost eight and a half, that a man could stand on the bottom anywhere in Wolf Lake, even in the middle, and the water would only be up to his neck. I had also heard that on a few occasions while sailing his small, tender sailboat on that windy lake, my uncle had done just exactly that.

Glen had been searching the horizon for any sign of a sail and making periodic checks of the public docks at Georgetown. Shortly after *Swan*'s lines were made fast at the quay, we had our long-awaited reunion. Glen and I had not seen each other for nearly 10 years, and he and Molly had never met.

Grand Cayman is an accommodating place. Any reasonable request is met with a positive response. The courteous and efficient port officials breezed us quickly through the formalities of entering port. Their British heritage was clearly evident.

During our three-day stay we strung new dacron lines on the self-steering servo and took care of laundry and other shoreside errands, traveling in the luxury of Glen's rental car. Money exchange was not a problem in the free port of Georgetown; there is a bank on every corner.

Glen was signed on as an Able-bodied Seaman in the Port Captain's records. It was a time-honored rating that he was to earn during a passage to Florida plagued by unfavorable winds, bedeviling currents, and nearly continuous squalls.

Although it was overcast, the first two days out were exhilarating tradewind runs. I was thankful for this, as it gave Glen an opportunity to acclimate to life on board a blue-water cruising boat under pleasant conditions. When we rounded Cabo San Antonio on the western tip of Cuba in the Yucatan Channel, the passage became more arduous, and Glen became acquainted with the joys of traveling third class. We expected to encounter headwinds on our northeasterly course, but the unpredictable current was far more difficult to deal with. I compensated for the easterly set indicated on the pilot chart, but it proved to be nonexistent. The noon fix showed us to be farther to the west than my reckoning, which made closing with the Florida coast even more difficult.

It was a slow affair, requiring constant vigilance in order to take advantage of every windshift, and to minimize the effects of the unfavorable ones. Our slothful progress was occasionally accentuated by one of those 500-knot airliners whizzing overhead.

Glen graduated from A.B. to Pilot as he guided *Swan* to the John's Pass drawbridge, which yawned open, admitting us into Florida's Inland Waterway.

I was dreading the Customs and Immigration clearing-in business. In view of all the places we had visited, and the length of time we had been out of the country, I'd prepared myself for a lengthy ordeal. After several telephone calls I reached an officer who handled affairs concerning yachts. He asked me a few desultory questions and then assigned *Swan* a clearance number, saying, "That's it, you're in. Welcome back." I was flabbergasted. I quickly hung up the telephone before he changed his mind.

In less than an hour we were approaching the condominium complex on Boca Ciega Bay, where Glen and my aunt Ruth live at the water's edge. They had invited us to stay as their guests during the hurricane season. Flags of the countries and island republics we had visited during the voyage were flying gaily from the backstay, with the United States ensign topmost. We were still a long way from home, but we were back in the U.S.A.!

15

WITH THE onset of the Caribbean hurricane season our attention turned toward the land, and travel upon it. To this end we purchased a second-hand Chevrolet. We tuned it, tinkered with it, waxed and polished it, and took great care not to mention a word about our newly acquired land yacht in the presence of *Swan*, our sensitive lady who was lanquishing in mothballs.

We planned to visit my family and relatives in Indiana and members of Molly's family in Missouri. With *Swan* in safe hands we set out for Indiana.

Even though we were aware of the runaway inflation that had occurred in the United States in our absence, it was still a shock to deal with it first-hand. Two items on our inflation-measuring yardstick, hamburger and gasoline, had doubled in price. In two stops at service stations we spent as much money for fuel as we had crossing the entire 6500-mile expanse of the Indian Ocean.

It was wonderful to see my family again. My mother loved the slides of our voyage, though I sensed she was still shaking her head to think that any son of hers would drag his bride out on the foaming brine in that little bitty boat.

A month later and 10 pounds heavier, we drove to Missouri. Our arrival there precipitated more family gatherings and more gathering around the midsection.

We weren't accustomed to eating so much while expending so little energy. At sea, one is constantly burning calories isometrically, bracing against the pitch and roll.

I became ill during this visit. Molly thought, with nurse's logic, that it was caused by an infectious virus. I preferred to believe that it was the effect of some insidious ex-infantryman's shock syndrome, brought on by being in the vicinity of Fort Leonard Wood, the army basic training post where I had spent a few miserable months in the winter of 1958, lugging a heavy pack and assorted weapons up and down the ice-covered hills of Missouri. Molly thought my diagnosis was a little weak medically, but as her tender feet had never worn army boots, I blithely disregarded her opinion. Sure enough, the malady cleared up at a rate that appeared, at least to me, to be in direct proportion to the widening distance between me and the scene of my earlier trials. We meandered through the Deep South back to St. Petersburg.

Waiting for us in Florida was a mysterious letter from Kenya. We didn't know anyone from Kenya. The address was hand-printed across the face of the envelope in large, uneven letters, obviously with some difficulty. I carefully and excessively examined the rumpled envelope to tease Molly, who was approaching her state of extreme anticipation. Finally I opened the letter, and was startled to see a stained, faded note that I recognized as my own handwriting:

> *Please refill and return to 17 degrees south latitude, 80 degrees east longitude, or better still, write me a letter to: (our home address). Bound for Port Louis, Mauritius, eleven days out of Christmas Island.*

> *Cheers!*   Jim Moore
> *Yacht* Swan
> *Sept. 8, 1979*

With the note was a letter from Gilbert Mwavuna Tembo, a 16-year-old boy who lived in Mombasa, an Indian Ocean seaport in Kenya. He had found the bottle we had thrown overboard in the central Indian Ocean. It had bobbed around on the high seas for nearly eight months before it washed ashore.

I wrote the following letter containing the facts of the bottle's drift to the Defense Mapping Agency in Washington, D.C.

Dear Sir:

In April of this year my wife and I touched back to the United States after a three-year voyage on our 36-foot sailboat, in which we circumnavigated the earth.

We periodically placed notes in bottles during the long passages, showing the latitude and longitude and our home address. We requested anyone finding one write us. To our surprise we received a letter from one Gilbert Mwavuna Tembo, from Mombasa, Kenya, this week. He found one of the bottles and wrote us.

The bottle was thrown overboard in the Indian Ocean at 17 degrees south latitude and 80 degrees east longitude on September 8, 1979. Gilbert found it on the beach at Mombasa on May 26, 1980, 230 days later. From information in his letter, I think the bottle was found in a fairly busy area of the beach, and probably did not lie there very long. On that assumption, the bottle made the 2500-mile trip in 230 days, averaging just under 11 nautical miles per day, which in a general way is in line with the information on the charts.

I might be offering covered-wagon methods in the space age, but it is pretty accurate information and might be of use to your department that deals with ocean currents and prepares those excellent pilot charts that we who are propelled by wind and current find so useful.

Plese write if you want any additional details, as I have Mr. Tembo's address.

Oh yes, a personal note. The bottle that Mr. Tembo found happened to be one that contained some rather good South Australian wine, used to celebrate my wife's 43rd birthday. How's that for a coincidence?"

> *Very truly yours,*
> *Jim Moore*
> *Yacht Swan*

In response, a naval officer with the Hydrographic Office wrote me a letter saying that the results of the bottle drift would be incorporated into the world surface current data base. My letter was published in the agency's newspaper, and I sent a copy to Gilbert. It must have been heady stuff for a teenage boy in Kenya to see his name in a newspaper that circulated through the halls of the Pentagon.

We continued to correspond with Gilbert over the succeeding years. He married, and a year later a son, Jim, my namesake, was born. Gilbert's letter announcing Jim's birth included a promise: "Don't worry Molly, your time will come." And indeed it did, the following year, when their daughter Molly was born. Grandkids nine and ten.

The cruising budget was in a sorry state. We had to revitalize it during the remaining months of the hurricane season. Molly was the first to find employment. She was hired as a waitress in a nearby restaurant, drawing on the experience that she gained in Sydney—only this restaurant actually had customers. Her uniform was in the style of an old-fashioned English maid, and she did very well at her job.

I found work with a painting contractor, scraping, sanding, and painting 300 outside lights and numerous fire doors in a high-rise condominium complex. The job redefined the word boredom. Work for pay has never excited me very much, dating back to my days as a skinny kid lugging a heavy leather bag full of golf clubs around the links under a broiling August sun in Indiana for two or three dollars a day. Building *Swan* was the only work I ever really enjoyed, and it had nothing to do with pay. Unfortunately, the economic scheme of things was designed without regard to my personal preferences, and the never-ending string of corroded lights and rusted fire doors was the piper demanding his due if the dance were to continue. So week after week I scraped and painted, occasionally looking seaward to where the horizon blended into the infinite sky. It was a siren's call, a palpable beckoning. I knew, then and there, that after this voyage my life would never again be the same.

It was autumn. In August, super-hurricane Allen had ripped a swath of death and destruction through the Caribbean. As the temperature gradually fell, the tropical storm threat decreased. The way was clear for the passage to Panama.

Swan was tugging at her moorings when we moved from the spacious luxury of my aunt and uncle's home to the compact living quarters on board the boat. In the last week of October, with fond farewells, we motored out of Boca Ciega Bay into the Gulf of Mexico, bound for Panama.

After a balky start a fresh breeze piped up out of the northeast, giving us three glorious days of running before the wind like an express train. But the train derailed a few miles south of Cabo San Antonio at the western tip of Cuba. Squalls assaulted us relentlessly for two days, causing radical changes in wind direction and velocity, and requiring nearly constant vigilance and many sail changes. Finally, to our dismay, the wind settled in from the south, blowing 20 to 25 knots.

Our increasingly dubious plan was to sail between the Quito Sueno and Serrana Banks. These reef-strewn shoals lurking off the east coast of Honduras are 35 miles apart, with a swift current running between them, and marked by unreliable navigational lights. The banks lay 200 miles southeast of our position, which would make it a rough slog to windward, with leeway adding to the worrisome problem of threading this potentially hazardous needle. However, I couldn't think of any reasonable alternative to closehauling the sails and pressing on to weather.

Molly felt, with ample justification, that we had experienced enough beats to windward to last a lifetime. That was precisely my feeling, but it didn't alter the situation. I pointed out this fact to the mate.

"But that's two or three days of Hellish Thrash!" she protested.

We had long ago discarded the traditional Beaufort Scale of Wind in favor of one of our own invention to decribe conditions when beating to windward. For example, Force 5 is Bone Jarring; Force 6 is Hellish Thrash, and above Force 6 the descriptions are too coarse to print.

"If it gets too rough we'll ease the sheets and bear off a bit until it's only Bone Jarring," I said in an effort to placate her.

While the less-than-placated mate looked on, I took a soft-lead pencil and dramatically scribed a thick black rhumbline on the chart squarely between the banks. Then I stomped up the companionway ladder and in a booming voice that would befit the weatherbeaten captain of a four-masted Cape Horner, I roared into the wind, "Stand by the lee braces! Close haul 'em for the weather leg when the topgallants back—look lively now!"

After a fruitless wait for the sound of feet pounding up the fo'c'sle ladder and the creaking of capstans, I went below and found a note lying on the chart table: "A gentleman never goes to windward."

"Well I guess that tells you something about me that you never knew before," I said, as I wadded up the note and threw it over the transom.

The seas were building as we sheeted in the sails. I adjusted the steering vane to the dreaded little mark scratched on the frame that would bring *Swan* up full and by. It took about 10 seconds for the boat to settle in on her new course and begin a hammering slog that would last for 50 hours.

The mate used these last peaceful moments to commandeer the leeward bunk. Her act, if not mutinous, was at the very least unsportsmanlike. It was then that I noticed that her toenails were painted and none of her fingernails was broken or even chipped—clearly the manifestations of decadence from living the soft life on the land. But being the good sailor that she is, she rallied about and whipped up a one-pot-to-weather-dish for supper while *Swan* plowed through the rough white water toward the banks.

As there was no possibility of reaching the banks during that first night, physical comfort was our main focus. However, on the second day of running on pure dead reckoning under heavy overcast skies, anxiety about our position had supplanted concerns of comfort. If we were not able to verify the DR by nightfall, I would stop the boat and wait until we could.

In the late afternoon I was nodding over a wordy tome chronicling every nuance of the American Civil War when I became drowsily aware of a shaft of sunlight streaming through the port. Sextant in hand, I bolted up the ladder, nearly scaring the wits out of the mate who was dozing in her posh bunk. We fell off the wind a couple of points to lessen the motion and allow me to get a fairly accurate sun sight. By chance it turned out to be the best possible observation in the circumstances. Moments after I took the sight the sun disappeared behind the clouds, not to appear again that day.

To appreciate the unique value of this celestial observation, a review of one aspect of an earlier discussion in this book on lines of position might be useful. One LOP tells the navigator that the ship is somewhere on that line. It requires a second LOP to fix the exact position where the two lines cross. What made this particular sun sight so advantageous was that the sun popped out from behind the clouds at the precise moment that its azimuth, or direction from us, was exactly 90 degrees to our course. The resulting LOP was parallel to the rhumbline and only a couple of miles away. We weren't sure where Vine Street was, but at least we knew we were still driving down Hollywood!

An acquaintance of ours, whose navigational skills are better than his command of the King's English, explains it this way: "One line of position don't tell you where you are exactly, but it tells you where you ain't." In other words, my sight told us we were not near the shoals, and that *Swan* was, in fact, approaching the banks nearly dead center, right on my fat, penciled rhumbline!

On the following morning an officer on a northbound British ship peered electronically through the murky sky and gave us our position by satellite fix. We were south of the shoals and just a few miles out of our reckoning.

Safely through the rocks and reefs, I looked into the eyes of my loving wife and uttered the three little words she was longing to hear: "Ease the sheets."

President-elect Ronald Reagan's voice came through the earphones as I sat in the companionway listening to a Voice of America broadcast of a press conference in the early morning on the fifteenth day of the passage. I absently noted the morning twilight illuminating the southern sky. Southern sky! The sun doesn't do things like that! It must be Cristobal, or neighboring Colón! But why were the lights visible at such a great distance? These towns were relatively small, yet they lit up the sky like a major city.

A round of morning star-sights fixed our position 50 miles north of Cristobal. If the wind held we had a good chance of arriving before nightfall. Molly sighted land just before noon.

An easterly setting current of one knot was indicated on the pilot charts in the approaches to Cristobal. Three knots was closer to the mark. We had not allowed for such a strong current, and *Swan* was set well to the east as we closed with the land. A frustrating ordeal followed. Cristobal and the eye of the wind were as one. It was an uphill battle, and to avoid the full force of the current we tacked well in toward shore, then put about on a short seaward leg, making up toward the harbor entrance in the late afternoon.

When darkness fell we were still several miles away. It was then that we discovered the source of the "city lights." More than 60 ships were anchored in the roadstead outside Cristobal Harbor, nearly all of them fully lighted. The lights of Cristobal and Colón were barely visible behind this spectacular panorama.

Steering fully 20 degrees to starboard of our course to compensate for the swift current, we motored through the cluster of ships, maintaining a sharp lookout for stray lines and cables. With no small measure of relief we passed through the open arms of the breakwaters and entered the safe haven of Cristobal Harbor.

Swan's anchor chain rattled through the hawse and shattered the tranquility of the "flats", as the small-craft anchorage is known. We were anchored in what had been, until 1977, the Canal Zone. The canal treaty between the United States and Panama had given immediate, though partial control of the canal to the Panamanians. The Americans were leaving; there was no Canal Zone now—it was all Panama.

It was serene in the anchorage. I leaned wearily against the dodger, thinking of the great physical exertion, expense, and engineering genius that had brought the canal into existence; the culmination of the efforts of so many people, from the rank-and-file laborers toiling in the humid tropical heat, to an indomitable American chief of state. Now this triumph was passing into Panamanian ownership. It was probably the right thing, but for a fleeting moment I thought I heard Teddy Roosevelt turn over in his grave.

We stayed for a week at the Panama Canal Yacht Club while we organized for the trip through the canal. In addition to a pilot we needed four line-handlers and a helmsman on board. We solved the line-handler problem by hiring two American fellows on a nearby yacht, and a lively young Panamanian, Anthony, who approached everything he did with boundless enthusiasm.

Gilbert, our Panamanian pilot, came on board on the morning that we were scheduled to transit the canal. He inspected our lines and questioned me about how I intended to use them. When he was satisfied that everything was in order he gave me permission to proceed toward Gatun Locks.

These locks raise a vessel in three steps to the level of Gatun Lake, a large, man-made lake 85 feet above sea level. The *Gulf Queen*, a ship from Wilmington, Delaware, had just entered the lock. We entered behind her and were immediately overwhelmed by our surround-ings. It was as if we were a toy sailboat in a bathtub.

The locks measure 1000 feet in length and are 110 feet wide. At each end of the lock are two enormous gates, hinged vertically. When opened, they fit flush into recesses in the lock walls. The gates are activated by massive steel operating arms that also disappear into the walls. The gates are honeycombed in such a way that air can be pumped into them to displace the water, enabling them to be floated to a dry dock for maintenance.

Gravity-fed water from Gatun Lake enters the lock through a system of culverts equal in size to the train tubes that pass beneath the Hudson River. From these main culverts, 20 smaller lateral tubes extend under the chamber, distributing the water through 100 inlets, each measuring four and a half feet in diameter. The average time required for a lock to fill is seven minutes. The greater a ship's displacement, the faster the lock fills.

I declined an offer to tie alongside a tugboat, reason-ing that even the most conscientious tugboat skipper can easily damage so delicate a charge as a 36-foot sailboat. Gilbert agreed, and we center-tied *Swan* in the chamber.

Men high above on the lock walls heaved light lines to us, which we tied to four heavy lines each measuring at least 100 feet in length. The port and starboard bow lines were led up and forward to their respective sides of the chamber, and the stern lines were led up and aft in the same manner. The lines were fastened to large bol-lards on top of the walls. We reeved the lines through blocks to the winches, which enabled us to take up on them in an orderly fashion as the chamber filled.

Molly was stationed at the tiller, and the two young Americans handled the stern lines. I managed one of the bow lines so that I was in a position to observe the entire operation and still hear Gilbert's instructions.

Anthony, who had made the canal transit many times, handled the other bow line.

The huge gates swung slowly shut behind us. When closed they formed an inward obtuse angle which buttressed them against the pressure of the water.

Fresh water from Gatun Lake coursed through the conduits, boiling into the chamber. *Swan* surged at her lines as the powerful flood of water buffeted her, illustrating the wisdom of assigning a man to each mooring line. As the water level rose the turbulence decreased accordingly. Our trusty crew took in the mooring lines while keeping a light strain on them to maintain our central position in the lock.

The ponderous gates of the second lock opened, allowing us to enter the next chamber. At this point Gilbert spoke by portable VHF radio to the pilot of the *Gulf Queen*, reminding him that a sailboat was astern of him. The reason for this soon became clear. Railroad engines, called mules, tow the ships through the locks. To assist the mules in overcoming inertia, the ship captains "kick" their propellers ahead, and the resulting wash can wreak havoc on small craft locking through behind them. Gilbert was on top of his job throughout the transit.

With the first set of locks astern, we motored into Gatun Lake. The 31-mile route across the lake to the first lowering lock, Pedro Miguel, is well-marked. A fresh breeze was blowing across the lake. Gilbert, who had settled himself into a corner of the cockpit with his newspaper and a beer, suggested that we hoist a sail. We hanked on the reacher and were soon power sailing at seven knots.

Nine miles from Pedro Miguel, Gatun Lake ends and Gaillard Cut begins. This waterway passes through the continental divide, between banks exceeding 300 feet in height in some areas. From this section of the canal alone, 230 million cubic yards of soil and rock were excavated—a volume equivalent to a 12-foot-square shaft cut through the center of the earth. Gaillard Cut is named after Colonel David Gaillard, who was in charge of this part of the canal's construction.

We entered Pedro Miguel lock with *Royal Fornax*, a Liberian-registered ship, and were lowered 31 feet to Miraflores Lake. Our jackrabbit start out of the lock put us ahead of the lumbering *Royal Fornax*. We crossed the mile-long lake and entered Miraflores Lock. *Swan* was in the forward part of the chamber, and we had the disconcerting sensation of being trapped in a cylinder with a piston inexorably coming toward us—*Gulf Queen* being the piston. The "mules" stopped her a short distance away, with her bow towering above us. Someone pulled the plug, and in two steps we descended 54 feet to sea level. Once again the great doors opened. Before us lay the Pacific Ocean.

At Balboa, four miles from Miraflores Locks, a Canal Commission launch came alongside and Gilbert left us. Fortified with hamburgers, our three crew members went ashore at the Balboa Yacht Club fuel dock. From Balboa, they rode the Panama Railroad passenger train back to Cristobal.

All canal tolls are levied on a net tonnage basis, which is determined by a special Panama Canal measurement system. Yachts are not required to pay a surcharge; therefore they transit at rates that constitute one of the greatest bargains ever. Our total fee was $17.29. I'm sure it was a different story with *Swan*'s locking companions.

Richard Halliburton paid the lowest transit toll, 36 cents, when he swam the Canal in 1928. On the other end of the scale, the *Queen Elizabeth II* paid a whopping $89,154.62 on her seventh transit in January 1980.

Thirty five miles east-southeast of Balboa lies the

Archipelago de Las Perlas, and in this group is a small island, Contadora, that became well known internationally when Panama granted political asylum to the shah of Iran. For a short time the island was his residence. We decided to go there to see for ourselves how your average shah had lived in exile.

My sense of direction was temporarily destroyed during the canal transit. The Isthmus of Panama is shaped like a letter S, tilted to the northwest. The canal is cut through the middle section of the S, and follows a northwesterly to southeasterly direction. Therefore, a vessel bound westward from the Atlantic side proceeds *southeast* to get to the Pacific side. I never really sorted it all out, and was at the point of believing that some cataclysmic event had upset the cosmos while we were in the bowels of the locks; that the sun would rise forevermore over the North Pole.

Fortunately this directional vortex had no ill effects on the mate, and she navigated us to Contadora as if there were yellow lines marking the route.

16

WIND IS such a rare and whimsical entity in the
Gulf of Panama that it is difficult to determine
logically when or from what direction it will
blow. Fickle winds are merely a nuisance while sailing,
but they constitute a dangerous threat to a boat lying at
anchor at an island where no shore can safely be assumed
to be on the leeward side. An onshore wind can pipe up
quickly in the middle of the night and turn a snug
anchorage into a living nightmare. At Contadora we
gambled on a small bay facing the mainland.

The natural forces that are so penurious with the
wind are more than generous with the gulf's diurnal tide
range, and this compounded our anchoring problems.
We anchored with a ratio of anchor chain to water depth
calculated at high tide. I dove and checked the set of the
anchor—a pleasant task in the warm, clear water of the
gulf.

Swan was anchored about a half-mile as the crow
flies from a posh resort that the deposed Iranian leader
frequented during his stay on the island. The journey
wouldn't have been bad for a crow, but the rugged terrain
posed a problem for us, as we would be wearing dress
clothing in order to crash the party that surely must be
going on at the resort.

The hard dinghy was packed full of lifesaving gear,
so we decided to use the "four-man" inflatable—a rubber
dinghy that would give three pygmies fits of claustro-

phobia. One of the more annoying traits of the miserable thing was its tendency to ship water at every opportunity, drenching its occupants from the waist down. With this in mind we boarded it wearing bathing suits and carried our clothing in plastic bags. This precaution proved to be wise, as the wretched dinghy reconfirmed its lowly reputation during the row to the beach.

We dressed at the water's edge and set off through the bush, picking our way carefully along a path that was in the final stages of a losing battle with the encroaching underbrush. For a brief moment I wondered about the return trip in the dark. I was well aware that we were putting a disproportionate amount of stock in the small flashlight Molly carried on excursions such as this one.

After several twists, turns, and confusing switch-backs, our path crossed a fairly well-used trail that appeared to lead toward the resort. I made a mental note that a tree with several gourd-like objects hanging from it marked the intersection of the two paths. I also noted, with some apprehension, that although I was only a few feet from the path leading back to the boat I couldn't see it, and it was still daylight.

The serpentine trail eventually brought us near enough to the resort that we were able to hear voices. We left the path when it seemed to be veering away from the complex, and stumbled through the thicket toward the distant noise and laughter. Slightly disheveled, we emerged as casually as possible from the jungle. I surreptitiously broke a limb of a small tree to mark the spot, thinking as I did so that Hansel's method of marking a trail with bread crumbs had more going for it.

Feigning an air of two aloof yuppies on vacation, we entered the lounge and seated outselves at a table near a large, elegant dining room. We instantly felt underdressed and underfinanced.

Molly had been perusing the menu for only a few seconds when a waiter appeared in a smart cummerbund and a black suit with shiny lapels.

"The gentleman and the lady will be dining this evening?" he asked, as if we might have information about another couple.

I glanced at Molly, who had put down the menu as if it were contaminated with the pox. She was giving me the how-do-we-get-out-of-here look.

"No, thank you," I said. "The lady and I will have two beers."

Sniffing a condescending acknowledgement, the waiter scooped up the menus and swished away toward the bar.

A fact of life had suddenly become vividly clear to us. There are places in this world where a shah dines, and places where we dine. This was definitely not one of our places.

We were sipping the beer and discussing our next move when an elderly gentleman at a nearby table turned to us. He apologized for listening to our conversation and asked if we were Americans or Canadians. I answered his question and invited him to join us, which he did.

Hans was his name. He was Scandinavian by birth, living in Colombia, where he owned a business. He came to Contadora three or four times each year on holiday. He told us that his wife had died four years earlier; that he was a lonely man, and would rather not dine at all than dine alone. We would be his guests for dinner, and he would not listen to any arguments to the contrary. I don't believe I could have thought of a plausible argument in a week.

Hans was a fascinating, enigmatic man. His vague account of his business dealings in Colombia did nothing to lessen this aura of mystery. A wealthy Scandinavian living in South America—it smacked of international intrigue. I had to fight back my Walter Mitty instincts.

He was familiar with some of the shah's activities during the monarch's stay at Contadora. The shah lived in a secluded villa, and periodically he and his entourage dined in kingly style at the resort. On these occasions the dining room was cleared of all other patrons, and his bodyguards were stationed at the doors with machine guns. Not surprisingly, this high-handed treatment did not sit well with the regular customers and the resort had suffered in the long run.

The dining room had closed and just a few stragglers were at the bar when we bid our unusual friend good night and started toward the boat. "Toward" was the operative word. There wasn't a ghost of a chance of finding the branch that I had so cleverly broken to guide the way. I could barely see Molly, who was only a few feet behind me. We groped through the dense flora until by some undeserved stroke of luck we found the well-used path. The sickly yellow beam of the flashlight, which had been deprived of first-echelon maintenance for the past decade, struggled to pierce the veil of darkness, only dimly illuminating our immediate surroundings.

"Look for a tree with about six gourds on it," I said, wishing I had skipped that last brandy.

Every tree was laden with them! Searching for the intersecting path was becoming an exercise in hopelessness. Reluctantly we set off through the trailing vines and underbrush by dead reckoning. Insects swarmed around us in the humid, cave-like blackness. I tried to dismiss my thoughts of the slithering, venomous reptile that might be lurking just ahead, poised to strike with bared fangs. I was now wishing that last brandy had been a double.

With a surge of relief I saw *Swan*'s masthead light through an opening in the brush—at eye level. About 50 feet below us, down a steep bank, gentle waves lapped at the shore. We slalomed our way down the bank and crashed onto the beach.

Off came the evening finery. It wasn't quite so fine anymore. For the return trip in the dinghy I never bothered to put on my swimsuit, but Prim and Proper did. Thanks to the evil inflatable we were thoroughly cooled off by the time we climbed aboard *Swan*.

We sat for a while enjoying the balmy breeze and talked about this most unusual evening. The anticipation of experiences such as this one had been our prime motivation during the boatbuilding days; those back-to-back months and years of work that drew sustenance from dreams. This spontaneous evening; this chance meeting of an interesting person on a small island, like ships passing in the night, is to a large degree what cruising is all about.

On the following morning, late, we sailed for Costa Rica. The information contained in *Ocean Passages For The World* was not what we wanted to read:

> Bound in any direction from Panama, the chief difficulty is the passage out of Panama Bay, for the light and baffling winds or calms are met with there in all seasons... the passage to ports along the coast of Central America is slow and troublesome to sailing vessels; advantage must be taken of every shift of wind to get to the northwestward.

The passage began under fair skies, with a favorable wind that belied the dour prediction in the sailing directions. *Swan* cut swiftly through the smooth water, banishing all pessimistic thoughts. After all, we were back in the grand Pacific. *Swan* knew about this place, her old stamping-grounds, and we were running for home. Then, off Point Mala on the Azuero Peninsula the wind died, never to be resurrected for the remainder of the passage, except for a few brief periods when an impotent breeze sparked a futile hope in our sailors' hearts. There were 250 miles of ocean between us and our destination, Golfito, a small town on Golfo Dulce in Costa Rica—a long 250 miles.

Ships from everywhere in the North Pacific, bound to and from the Panama Canal, pass near the Azuero Peninsula. One or more were always visible in that area during the day or night.

It was about an hour before morning twilight. We were closehauled on the starboard tack, making off the land with a light northwest wind that had been blowing, timorously, for part of the night. Our plan, if the wind held, was to change tacks at sunrise and sail through a wide channel at the western tip of the peninsula between Isla Coiba, an island about 20 miles long, and the mainland. This was the most direct route to Golfito, and there were several good anchorages along the way.

I was on watch and had been observing a ship about a mile ahead of us, running in a southerly direction, roughly at right angles to our course. Another ship was overtaking us with the apparent intention of passing on our port side. I was concerned about this because we were hard on the wind and had no means of maneuvering to starboard without tacking. The overtaking ship was clearly the burdened vessel in regard to both *Swan* and the ship crossing ahead, though right-of-way never influenced our thinking for a moment when dealing with ships at sea. However, the person on watch on the ship ahead of us was concerned about it.

A terse message spoken in clipped words crackled over the VHF radio from the southbound ship, intended for the vessel overtaking us: "Observe the rules of the road." The burdened ship responded immediately by turning about 20 degrees to starboard, putting us in instant jeopardy as less than 400 yards separated us. The ship's range lights were nearly in line, and I could see both her red and green running lights—a replay of the frightening encounter with that ship in the South Atlantic.

It wasn't clear if the helmsman intended to pass close aboard on our port side, or even that he had seen us, even though we were well-lighted. There was no time to spare. I put the helm down and brought *Swan*'s bow through the eye of the wind. True to the infallible laws of Murphy, a forceful gust hit us just at the moment the sail was backwinded hard against the port spreader. The shock was too much for the old reacher—it ripped from leech to luff. The shredded sail flailed in the wind while the huge black hull throbbed past about 80 yards to port.

We had lost our number-one mileage maker. Under jib and main we poked along toward Isla Coiba, which was now visible in the gray light of dawn. But as the sun rose the wind died, and *Swan* sat motionless on the shimmering sea, 10 miles offshore, for the entire day. Near sundown we motored toward a tiny coastal island that appeared on the small-scale chart to have an inlet suitable for anchoring.

Night had fallen by the time we reached the island. I stood on the bow pulpit with a hand-held searchlight, looking for coral heads as we crept into the small bay, which was no more than 200 yards wide. Vegetation grew nearly to the water's edge, indicating that the bay was not exposed to high surf—not that we expected any in this millpond. We dropped the anchor in 20 feet of water.

I played the light across the water surrounding the boat to make certain there were no outcroppings of rock in our swinging radius. Flash! Something shot through the water near the surface at an astounding speed. We were peering into the water when a sleek silver fish, approximately four feet in length, burst through the surface and struck the side of the boat. Molly scrambled onto the dinghy on the cabintop, letting out a shriek that should have been sufficient to repel boarders of any species—but not this fish. Barracuda are not easily frightened.

In the glare of the spotlight the fish executed two amazing high-speed left turns and from about 50 feet it made a lightning charge at the boat, exploding out of the water with its mouth wide open and teeth bared, striking the rubrail just six inches below the deck. Molly shrieked again, and I fell backward across the cabintop, where I remained until this ferocious fish grew tired of banging its head against the hull.

I have an indelible picture in my mind, a freeze frame of that mouthful of pointed teeth, like an attacking Doberman, flying through the air in the brilliant light.

The mate saw little humor in my suggestion that she dive and check the set of the anchor. It was all I could do to get her to come down from her perch atop the dinghy.

Golfo Dulce is a placid narrow inlet, 25 miles long and eight miles wide, with protected anchorages in abundance. We were ghosting along near the shore when we saw a freshwater stream cascading down a lushly foliated hillside, emptying into the ocean in a small cove with swaying palms and a white sand beach. One doesn't pass by an anchorage like this, even at ten o'clock in the morning within two hours of one's destination! It was a perfect place to swim, bathe, wash our clothes, lie in the sun, and wonder what everyone else in the world was doing.

Unfortunately our memories of Costa Rica took an unfavorable turn after this pleasant stop. *Swan* was broken into and burglarized while we were spending an evening ashore at Golfito. The thieves made off with two shortwave radios, two chronometers, a pair of binoculars, a sailbag full of new running rigging, and miscellaneous articles. The police did not consider the matter worthy of investigation. It probably would have done little good anyway, but their attitude did nothing to assuage our feelings of being violated.

The immediate problem was navigation. Luckily, the locker where the sextant was stowed had been overlooked; however, the navigational use of a sextant is greatly diminished without the ability to keep time. A travel alarm clock was the only timepiece on board the boat. An old tin clock might have been good enough for Joshua Slocum, but we had been spoiled by precision quartz chronometers and radio time-ticks—essential elements of accurate high-seas navigation.

Golfito was not exactly a center of commerce. There was no hope of finding what we needed in this small, provincial town. After making a few inquiries, we learned that we might have luck at a border town between Costa Rica and Panama, about 50 miles from Golfito. We boarded a slow-moving bus packed with people carrying squawking chickens and squalling babies for a nerve-racking ride along narrow, winding mountain roads to reach the Panamanian frontier.

We stepped off the bus into the street that was the boundary between the two countries. On the Costa Rican side was a row of plain, drab buildings; on the Panamanian side, modern buildings with flashing neon signs and display windows crammed full of the latest electronic items from all parts of the world. In one of the bustling stores we found a shortwave radio receiver that appeared to have the frequency bands we needed to pickup the broadcast of Greenwich Mean Time. I wanted to test the radio outside, away from the interference inside the store. The clerk was confused about my intentions. He glanced furtively about as if he were looking for assistance to prevent this crazy gringo from taking the radio without paying for it.

Delving into my 92-word Spanish vocabulary I said, "Fuera tranquila, por favor." while alternately pointing at the radio and toward the street.

"Si."

"Gracias."

We walked out into the street and I tuned in WWV, the time station, and heard the reassuring sound of a distant voice announcing the correct time.

A quartz wristwatch completed the shopping requirements, and we boarded a bus for the trip back to Golfito.

With the radio in place, *Swan*'s navigational systems were fully operational. Her primary means of propulsion wasn't. Two full days were spent repairing the torn reacher with an ancient, hand-cranked sewing machine we had purchased secondhand in Fiji.

Our longest passage of the voyage, 4350 nautical miles of blue Pacific, lay between *Swan* and Honolulu. We had decided against the idea of sailing the direct route northward along the North American coast to Portland. The prospect of endless motoring in windless Central American waters, and the thought of enduring chilly, hazardous fog and adverse winds along the California and Oregon coasts, were more than we cared to consider. Besides, one doesn't need much justification for wanting to run the westing down in the heart of the trades to spend some time in the Hawaiian Islands. The immediate problem was how to get through the exasperating calms extending well off the Mexican coast.

"NEXT STOP Hawaii Yacht Club," I shouted from the foredeck as I fine-tuned the set of the patched reacher in a Force 4 southeaster that had sprung up out of nowhere. Don't question it! Run for the open sea while it lasts! Broad reaching at six knots, chasing the setting sun—we're rolling west! If I did it a thousand times, I doubt that I would ever become inured to the feeling of exhilaration of running before a favorable wind at the beginning of a passage, distancing myself from the rules and restraints of land things; accepting the risks and hardships that are part of the price of independence, but also enhance the freedom.

Day 3: Christmas Day, 1980. I made a Christmas card for Molly. On the cover was a drawing of *Swan* under full sail in rugged seas. Sitting askew on the cabintop was a sleigh, and in it was a rotund, jolly Santa. Reindeer were draped over the lifelines, piled on the deck, and tangled in the rigging. A voice coming from below deck said: "I don't care who you are fat man, get those reindeer off my foredeck!"

Much to our surprise the wind had held fairly steady, giving us average daily runs of just over 100 miles. It was a psychological lift, given the enormous expanse of water stretching before us. My mistake was in logging them on the chart—Three little X-marks, struggling to get away from the land.

Day 8: Dead in the water for most of the night. With

the sunrise came the wind from the northeast, gently, but with authority. It increased steadily during the morning hours, settling in at an optimum Force 5. Could we possibly have reached the trades so soon? I wasn't even sure they existed in the winter. But if it looks like a duck, and it walks like a duck, and it quacks like a duck...

Day 12: For the two preceding days *Swan*'s speed through the water had been at odds with the distance run between celestial fixes. I reworked the sights and Molly checked my calculations. There were no errors. At midday I crossed the customary running fix on the sun with an additional LOP from the moon, establishing a very reliable position. In the evening we took a round of star-sights. During the six hours that had elapsed between fixes, *Swan* had maintained a 5½ knot average speed through the water, which should have placed her 33 miles down the track. The actual distance run between fixes was 24 miles. Apparently she was bucking a 1½-knot current. It was perplexing, because the pilot chart for December showed the equatorial countercurrent to be well south of our position. Nevertheless, a current existed, and it was costing us a lot of miles. We altered course 20 degrees to the north and maintained it for two days until we ran out of the adverse flow of water.

Day 14: 1485 miles west of Puntarenas, Costa Rica. A small bird landed on the dodger. Typical of most seabirds, it showed no fear when I approached it. I placed my hand under its breast and it stepped into my palm. I then noticed a band fitting loosely around its spindly leg, and recorded the number. Later, in Honolulu, we sent a letter to the Audubon Society with the band number and the location of the bird at the time of the sighting. We received a certificate of appreciation from the U.S. Fish and Wildlife Service, stating that the bird, a common tern, was banded in Ithaca, New York six months earlier when it was too young to fly.

That afternoon, on my daily inspection of the rigging and running gear, I noticed several small tears along the stitching of the repaired reacher. Sunlight shone through the needle perforations, which were closer together than they should have been, further weakening the tired old sail. I knew it was only a matter of time until it would happen, like the words on a cereal box: "Tear on dotted line."

Day 16: 14°7'N, 112°47'W. Another time zone down. We set the clocks back one hour, and were now eight hours slow on Greenwich Mean Time. Squalls were visible in every direction. We ran up the loose-footed storm trysail with the tack tied to a shroud, forming a loop at the foot of the sail. As the squalls came through, one after another, the deluge of rainwater ran down the sail and poured into a five-gallon bucket suspended from the boom. We collected enough water to top off the main freshwater tank and wash the bedding. In the late afternoon the weather cleared enough for us to string lines fore and aft to dry the sheets. Folded in half over the line, with six clothes-pins per sheet, they flew horizontal in the strong wind and dried in 20 minutes. An entry in the log read "Flying every rag on board."

Day 18: This day began, more or less, like any other—until The Bird arrived.

I hesitate to recount this tale for three reasons: one, the book is at risk of becoming top-heavy with bird stories; two, I do not want to agitate the Audubon Society, particularly after receiving a certificate of appreciation for our avian achievements; and three, the account could be regarded as bizarre, suggesting, perhaps, that the author "went around the bend" as the British say, and putting a strain on my credibility as a teller of true tales. But it happened this way, and certain stories should be told regardless of the consequences.

My watch was over. A beautiful sunrise with a clear

horizon and a Force 5 quartering wind promised a relaxing day and a marking off of miles. The fish lines were out and the coffee was perking when I saw the spots—purple inkspots the size of silver dollars, one on deck and the other near the mast. As I was leaning down to make a closer examination, a loud squawk nearly scared the wits out of me. On top of the dinghy sat a bird the size of a large sea gull. A long yellow beak protruded from a black head with a sleepy, unblinking eye that stared intently at me. Its body was white with gray wings, and was supported by skinny legs with comical knobby knees and large webbed feet hooked over the chine of the dinghy. Any question as to the cause of the spots was put to rest when this brazen visitor made a purple deposit that ran down the white side of the dinghy. Apparently it lived on squid.

A bucket of seawater sloshed on the spots was to no avail. Detergent wouldn't touch them. It required a stiff brush and scouring powder, followed by bleach. I looked up from my labor just in time to see a fresh blob of purple running down the side of the dinghy. This bird had to move on.

I slapped the end of the dinghy with a wet towel and shouted "Go!" The bird didn't bat an eye. However, the commotion did bring the mate scrambling on deck from a sound sleep. She had a what-the-hell-is-going-on look on her face.

"I can't make this stupid bird get off the boat," I said lamely.

The mate just stood there staring, first at me, then at the bird, who stared alternately at each of us as it made another deposit on the dinghy.

To my chagrin, the feathered intruder showed no fear whatsoever when I picked it up. Using both hands I launched it into the air to leeward, as one shoots a basketball. It flew in a tight circle like a living boomer-ang and landed back on the dinghy.

Thoroughly annoyed, I slammed my fist down hard on the bottom of the boat about six inches from the bird. It hopped straight up in the air, landed, made a side shuffle to the stern of the dinghy, and did its business again.

I snatched the bird up fairly roughly in one hand, which caused the mate to shout, "Don't you hurt that bird!"

"I'm not going to hurt this stupid bird, but it doesn't know that. It doesn't know that people hunt birds, and they shoot birds, and they kill birds!"

With that outburst the mate went below.

Lying on the deck, I leaned over the toerail as far as I was able and dropped the bird into the water. It turned a forward somersault, righted itself, and sat floating on the water with a slightly disheveled look. For a minute or two I watched it preening itself on the crests of the waves, then went below.

"The miserable wretch is gone," I said to the mate, who by now had taken the bird's side. "After you give me a hand scrubbing the boat, maybe you won't feel so sorry for the bird."

This Captain Bligh approach was not well-received by the mate. A 12-ounce, long-beaked bird was destroying our tranquil sail in the sun.

Before things had a chance to deteriorate further a familiar squawk came from the open leeward port. The bird was standing there looking in at us.

"He's back," exclaimed the mate, as if I were blind and deaf.

I could not help but notice that suddenly this bad penny had become a "he." It was too outrageous. We lay on the bunks laughing while the bird peered quizzically into the boat.

Molly watched me open the long coaming locker. "Don't you shoot that bird!"

"I'm not going to shoot him, I'm going to scare him."

He was back on his favorite perch, the dinghy, doing his thing. I aimed the rifle toward the horizon about a foot above its head and pulled the trigger. Bam! The bird cowered, tucking its head against its wing. Never before had I felt like such an unmitigated bully. The bird did show enough intelligence to be frightened, but I had quite literally fired my biggest gun, and he was still there. The blast had only made things worse. It had scared the purple out of him.

There was one gambit left, but it would have to wait until nightfall. The night would be dark, as there was no moon—a necessary element of my plan.

Several times during the afternoon the bird flew off on short excursions, apparently in search of food. There was little doubt in my mind that he was running on empty. During one of his absences I spread a towel on the dinghy to absorb the droppings, hoping he would not regard it as a welcome mat.

When the last glow of twilight had faded into darkness I shut off the main battery switch, completely blacking out the boat. With a flashlight in hand I approached the bird, shining the light in its eyes. It didn't faze him whatsoever. He stared into the beam for about a minute, and this, too, was part of my plan—to temporarily destroy his night vision. I picked him up, leaned down near the water, and dropped him. In the beam of the light he did another somersault and righted himself as before.

For two hours we kept all lights out, and I never switched the masthead light on until four hours had passed. He didn't return. My log entry for that day noted that the bird had violated every rule of modern warfare.

Day 23: "What happened to all of the onions?" The

mate's voice snapped me awake from my dozing in the cockpit. "We have only two left," she said.

She might as well have announced that we had two gallons of water left. Meals just don't happen on board *Swan* without onions, and we were barely past the halfway point! The sack of onions we'd brought on board in Costa Rica had certainly seemed adequate. For most passages it would have been. Rationing began—the time of Transparent Onion Slices.

This day held more surprises in store. The wind, now Force 6, had been holding steady for days, and as the fetch had increased so had the seas. Occasionally the reacher would back slightly when *Swan* was in a trough on the lee side of an unusually large sea, then fill with a snap when the boat rose on the wave. Ordinarily I would have paid little attention to these occurrences, but the delicate condition of the sail had raised my level of concern.

The blowout finally happened with worse results than I had envisioned. *Swan* slued off a few degrees to weather on the face of an extraordinarily large sea. Vane struggled manfully to correct, and averted a broach, but the shock of the back and fill was too much for the fragile reacher, and for the spliced whisker pole. The entire wind propulsion apparatus was destroyed simultaneously. One moment it was a white, billowing, driving sail, held rigidly in place by a spar and taut lines, and the next moment it was a useless, shredded, flapping rag, entangled with a bent and twisted mass of aluminum scrap. Like "The One-Hoss Shay" of Oliver Wendell Holmes, "it went to pieces all at once—all at once and nothing first—just as bubbles do when they burst."

Unlike that stormy night in the South Atlantic when the pole had first broken, this time it did not sever completely, and spared us the wild thrashing on the foredeck. We lashed the broken pole along the toerail and hanked on the working jib, using the boom as a whisker pole. *Swan* was making four knots under this arrangement, and as night was falling, we carried on with the jib alone.

Four knots was a one-third drop in speed, which translated into approximately a week added to the passage—assuming the wind held. That never went down very well, especially in light of the onion supply. The problem was how to increase the sail area without moving the driving effort too far aft and creating steering difficulties.

A few calculations showed that the combined sail areas of the working jib and storm jib were nearly as great as that of the reacher. But how to fly them was the question. Suddenly it came to me. The storm jib was the most rugged sail in *Swan*'s inventory; therefore it could be hoisted on the main halyard to the top of the mast, where the wind was strongest.

We tied one line to the tack and two lines to the clew. The line attached to the tack was fixed to the windward toerail two feet aft of the mast, and served as a downhaul. We trimmed the sail with a line reeved from the clew through a block at the end of the boom (which was now doing double duty as a whisker pole), and then through a toerail block to a sheet winch. The other sheet led down and aft to a block and tackle attached to a stern mooring cleat. We now had a chafe-free sail at the top of the mast, pulling like a mule without creating a wind shadow to interfere with the working jib. *Swan* resumed her six-knot pace.

Day 25: We were now 2750 miles west of Puntarenas, and Vane was still performing flawlessly. As cynical as it may sound, I could not help but think that his steadfast loyalty had something to do with his being an eye-witness to the sea anchor's three-mile dive to the bottom of the Indian Ocean.

Day 29: January 20, 1981. A big day in Washington.

We listened to Ronald Reagan's inauguration via short-wave radio, and cheered as the 52 Americans who had been held hostage in Iran were flown to freedom.

Day 33: Force 8 winds and giant seas, by far the largest we had ever encountered, pursued *Swan* on her run to the west. I was amazed that the cockpit had not been swamped. The stern had been designed with sufficient buoyancy to lift, just in time, as the huge seas slid beneath the boat. My concern was speed—too much of it. Several times we exceeded eight knots, a worrisome speed in fair conditions and a dangerous one in these conditions. I wanted no part of surfing down those white-crested, curling blue monsters. We took in the skysail and slowed to a more reasonable six knots.

In order to reduce *Swan*'s steep angle of descent into what were now foamy chasms between the combers, we changed course a few degrees to the north, putting the wind and seas forward of the quarter, thus making possible a more oblique entry into the troughs. This tactic had worked well during the gale in the Mozambique Channel, but, as is so often the case during a storm, this defensive response introduced a new threat: While we had reduced the risk of pitchpoling, we had increased the chances of broaching. I considered it to be a good trade-off. A full-on broach in high seas is extremely dangerous, but even the most horrifying consequence of a broach, a 360-degree rollover, pales in comparison to a boat flipping end-over-end, crashing onto the surface of the water upside down, mast and rigging carrying away, pots and pans hurtling through the cabin, with serious injuries almost a certainty and sinking and death all too possible.

It soon became clear that holding course in these violent conditions required the constant vigilance of a human. Vane's unswerving devotion to duty, while impressive, did not fully compensate for the fact that his head was stuffed full of aluminum. He had no way of perceiving that a dangerous situation was developing, and could only react to an actual change in apparent wind direction. A strong gust of wind coinciding at the right moment with a breaking sea could force the bow to windward and cause a broach. An alert helmsman can sense this potentially hazardous combination in time to fall off to leeward a point or two until the danger has passed. The task at hand was to find some way of tolerating life at the helm.

Flying spume was a chilly nuisance in winds now ranging at the Force 9 level. Crests of the quartering seas slammed against the hull, throwing spray into the air, and the howling wind blew it over the weathercloths, drenching the helmsman. About three blasts in the face was sufficient to set me thinking about a way to assist Vane without carrying this togetherness to the point of taking a bath with him.

I eased the jib sheet until the sail was on the verge of luffing, thus making it less efficient—a desirable effect in this instance, as it slowed the boat to a speed my nervous system could accept. Also, if the boat came up on the wind a few degrees the jib would luff, providing a hair-trigger signal to the helmsman that an immediate corrective response was required, but allowing sufficient time to avert a broach.

Molly tended the helm while I assembled a rigging arrangement that would allow us to keep *Swan* moving as safely as possible without subjecting us to unnecessary discomfort.

First I attached a two-part block and tackle between the tiller and a cleat on the windward coaming, with the fall leading down into the cabin and fastened to a post amidships with a slippery hitch for release in an emergency. A thick length of shock cord, doubled, and strung between the tiller and a leeward lifeline stanchion provided the counter-pull against the block and tackle.

I tensioned the shock cord and adjusted the tackle until the main rudder was in slight opposition to the steering vane. This removed all slack from the system and reduced the vane's mechanical reaction time, as the steering vane servo was perpetually resisting the main rudder's effort. Whenever the forces of nature became too great for the steering vane to handle alone, a tug on the fall brought the main rudder into play, assisting the vane. The companionway door needed to be propped open only a few inches to allow clearance for the line. With the exception of an occasional check of the horizon, we stood watch in the relative comfort of the cabin.

A long night passed with very little rest for either of us. The ocean was a frightening frenzy of white water and towering seas, many so peaked that they were unable to sustain their unstable shape: They broke like surf on a beach, sheeting the surface of the water with white foam in the pale moonlight. It was fairly obvious to me that Vasco de Balboa never spent a night like this when he was having a look at this place in 1513, because if he had, he surely would not have given it the name Pacific.

Day 34: The dawn, always welcome in fair or stormy weather at sea, brought with it a scene of chaos. As *Swan* rose on the crests of the waves, I had glimpses of a white maelstrom stretching from horizon to horizon and blending in with the clouds that encircled us, creating an illusion of being in the bottom of a great roiling punch bowl.

With apprehension I watched the display of destructive power around us. Down we would plummet into the valley between the monstrous seas; seas that seemed capable of swallowing us up at will. My tired brain took in the scene with a strangely calm detachment, as though we enjoyed some special dispensation that made us immune to the sea's wrath. Maybe I felt this way because of the boat. We certainly were not immune to anything, but we were sailing in a sturdy, well-found vessel that forgave us for our mistakes, which sometimes placed a heavy strain on her. The sea, on the other hand, forgives nothing. It ferrets out weaknesses and deals harshly with them. Fortunately, it had to deal with *Swan* first in order to have a go at her occupants. I laid my head on my arms on the top step of the ladder and fell asleep, standing, almost instantly. *Swan* carried on. If she came up on the wind I didn't know about it.

Day 35: To our immense relief the winds had diminished during the night to Force 6; which seemed by comparison to be a wafting breeze. The seas, while still mountainous, had lost their vicious appearance.

On this day, if the wind held, we would cross our outbound track. By my reckoning—and that was all it was, as the sextant hadn't been out of its box for two days—we would cross it sometime in the late afternoon or evening.

Just ahead on the chart were two small X-marks, 145 miles apart, showing the Oct 15th and 16th noon positions on our first passage to the Hawaiian Islands in 1977. To establish the point at which our present course would intersect the old track, I connected the two positions with a straight line.

I took a sun-sight at 0900, and another at 1030, crossing the second with the first as a running fix. The results of this fix and the noon latitude were advanced and crossed with a 1400 observation of the sun. Finally, with as much drama as I could muster, I declared to the mate that we would cross our outbound track at 1615, give or take a few milliseconds.

Champagne had been on ice since early morning. I washed the cockpit to remove the storm-tossed salt residue. As I was wiping the cockpit with a chamois I glanced over the port weathercloth and saw a ship on the horizon running on an eastward course.

I called the ship on VHF radio and the answer was immediate. We were in a state of high excitement about the cruising milestone about to occur, and I told the captain about it. His response was one of unexpected enthusiasm. Using his satellite navigation system and radar, he plotted our position as a verification. The position I'd calculated from celestial fixes was within two miles of the ship's electronic fix. With a cockiness born out of being within a stone's throw of proving unequivocally that the world is indeed round, I said to the mate, with the microphone off, "It appears that the navigation satellite is a couple of miles out of its orbit."

At the appointed time I taped the camera to the cabintop under the dodger and set the automatic shutter release. We juggled the bottle and glasses while holding a large printed sign explaining what it was all about. At 1615, precisely, we activated the camera and poured the champagne. Full circle—circumnavigation complete! Latitude 20°26'N, longitude 150°12'W.

Theoretically we were occupying the same piece of real estate, although it was a few thousand feet beneath us, that we had nearly three and a half years earlier. It was about at that spot, on that earlier passage, that I was pacing the cabin, engulfed in self-doubt about my ability to find the Hawaiian Islands.

Day 38: Ghosting along the north shore of Molokai in a near calm. The navigation light on the Kalaupapa Peninsula blinked reassuringly. Molly unearthed our little black-and-white television and placed it in the cockpit. We switched it on and caught Johnny Carson in the middle of his monologue. No doubt about it—we were back in civilization.

18

WHILE SLOWLY motoring in the basin in front of the Hawaii Yacht Club we received a pleasant surprise. Waving and calling to us from the dock was Linda Balcomb. We had lost track of the Balcombs and assumed they were in California. After we left New Zealand for Sydney, *Starshine* had sailed east, revisiting the Marquesas before returning to Hawaii. It was a gala reunion.

We stayed in Hawaii, working odd jobs until spring. Technically we had circumnavigated, yet a voyage around the world is really incomplete until the boat is tied up at the same dock from which it departed. One more crossing of the Pacific remained for *Swan* and her crew.

Approximately 600 miles north of Honolulu the Northeast Trades fade away. Getting through this belt of adverse wind is the major obstacle when sailing from Hawaii to the mainland of the United States, and it is usually overcome by sailing two unequal legs. The first leg begins in the lee of the island, at the Ala Wai small-craft harbor, and continues along the shoreline to Diamond Head. This takes about 25 minutes if you don't dawdle along the way, looking at the bikinis on Waikiki Beach. The second leg begins the moment the boat noses past Diamond Head into the Molokai Channel. This initiates a Hellish Thrash to windward for about a week, sailing as close to the wind as can be tolerated. I had no intention of subjecting us, or our boat, to that second leg.

I approached the problem on the premise that it didn't matter if any easting were made on the run out of the trades. The plan was simple: Get north as comfortably as possible without regard to longitude, and around latitude 30°N, look for something favorable going east. As expected, the first leg was a piece of cake. We arrived at the threshold of Leg Two slightly behind the average time, because I did a little loop along Waikiki while the mate was below making final preparations for the slog north.

For two hours we reached out into the Molokai Channel in short, choppy seas and 25 knots of wind, flying the working jib and storm trysail, the pair of veterans that would see us out of the trades. Neatly folded in the forepeak, reserved for lighter airs, was a spanking new reacher, made in Honolulu.

Ready about! I adjusted the steering vane to a close reach on the starboard tack, a point of sail that can easily be tolerated. *Swan* settled back into the task before her. The compass heading read about 350 degrees, and when adjusted for an 11-degree east magnetic variation we were sailing true north in a civilized manner.

For six days we held this point of sail, often headed more toward Japan than Portland, Oregon during the first two days of the passage. Then the trades veered east, as they often do in the summer, and Vane dutifully followed. On the afternoon of the seventh day we were plodding along in a light breeze, in the belt of variable winds. We were out of the tradewinds and had managed to gain four degrees of easting in the process. Two dorado joined us for dinner, and we could not have been more pleased with how we negotiated this usually troublesome phase of the passage to the mainland.

If you allow it to affect you, sailing in variable winds

can be exasperating. We had learned over the years, not without some difficulty, to view them as a coin-flip, and live with the results without fighting the problem.

After a few feints and false starts a fresh breeze settled in from the south. We set the new reacher, poled out to port with the reconditioned whisker pole, and ran directly toward the mouth of the Columbia River for three days before the wind faltered and died for 40 hours.

While Molly prepared one of her elaborate Becalmed Meals, I rigged a cockpit awning and made a few half-hearted stabs at an article I had been working on. Three years had elapsed since my first article had appeared in a sailing publication; an event that had spawned my grand vision of being the natural successor to Jack London. In the interim, just enough of my articles had been published to keep the spark of hope ignited.

I was undaunted by the conspicuous absence of literary agents clamoring for the opportunity to represent me. The dearth of proposals could easily be explained: I was not, after all, the easiest person to find. It is difficult to negotiate profitable deals with the czars of book publishing when one is stumbling through the jungles of Panama in the black of night, or to expect an agent to locate a budding author and present him with a lucrative contract when the author himself isn't sure where he is. Even as we sat there, motionless, a thousand miles from land, it was just possible that representatives of publishing houses were standing on the beaches of Oregon, eyes peeled for a speck of white; a glint of sunlight on a spar. One never knew.

When the wind came it was not what we'd been hoping for. Not only was it from the north, making our course close to the wind, but it was cold. It had literally been years since we had felt the need to wear coats. Molly, who claims that she is suffering hypothermia the moment the temperature drops below 80 degrees, had periodically worn her foul weather gear during the brisk weather, and it was in fair shape. I had rolled mine up in tight bundles and stowed it in a rubberized canvas bag in 1977, a few days out of San Francisco on the passage to Hawaii, and had not opened the bag since then. The trousers and jacket were black with mildew, and cracked when I unrolled them. I put them back in the bag to await the rubbish bin.

In the small hours of the morning on July 5, 1981, I stood in the cockpit, leaning on the dodger, steering with my legs, holding a cup of steaming coffee with both hands and enjoying its warmth and aroma on a chilly, damp, foggy night. Oregon, my Oregon, you must be close by.

A round of star-sights on the previous evening had shown us to be within striking distance of the coast, and I had a case of the closing-with-the-land jitters. Time and 36,000 nautical miles of sailing had not appreciably lessened my nervous reaction to being near land at night. Perhaps that was why we were still afloat.

At 0400 a flicker of light shone through the gloom. Steering toward it, I soon identified the flash of the navigation light of the Columbia River outer marker, five miles southwest of the river's treacherous bar.

Swan nosed into the transient berth at West Basin Marina in Astoria, where, four years earlier, a pair of very green freshwater sailors had noted with some apprehension that the water *Swan* was floating in contained a good measure of salt.

The saltwater-wash, freshwater-rinse cockpit baths were fine at sea, but not on land. Molly headed for the coin-operated showers and pay phone with a large handful of quarters. She returned much later, red as a cooked lobster, hypothermia in remission, and reported that all of the calls to family and friends had been made.

Our dear friend Chuck Schmiel is one of those rare

individuals who can organize things properly. No friends of his were going to build a boat, sail it around the world, and return home unnoticed! He put his special skills to work and organized a first-class homecoming.

Swan was to sail into view from around a bend in the river at the confluence of the Columbia and Willamette Rivers in Portland at 10 a.m. We had stopped for the night a few miles downriver, and were so excited that we were up and about at daybreak.

We arrived at the bend in the river two hours early and dropped the anchor along the shore, out of sight. A few minutes before the appointed time we were underway with the flags of 15 countries and island republics flying from the backstay. As we sailed around the bend in the river a small flotilla of boats surrounded us, filled with familiar and unfamiliar faces: Television and newspaper people were there, and it was a heady experience for two people who, prior to this voyage, had lived very ordinary lives.

Swan eased alongside the dock amid the cheers, the clicking cameras, and popping champagne corks—a stone's throw from the boathouse where a cygnet had blossomed into a swan.

Champagne was bubbling over my head and Molly was bubbling over, just as she had on the morning we had left, which now seemed so long ago, almost dream-like. But it was all real—we had lived our dream. I kissed Molly and said, "What in the world do we do next?"

EPILOGUE

~~~~~~~~~~~~~~~~

I PULLED THE dipstick from the bank account and it read "critically low." There's a time and place for everything, and surely this was the time to earn some money. But the place...

After a few weeks in Portland, we meandered down the Columbia River, taking three days to cover the 80 miles to Astoria, and once again sailed westward toward Hawaii.

Doug Balcomb's dipstick was on the dry side, too. He and I formed a small company in Honolulu (it's difficult to get much smaller than two guys and a rusty station wagon) repairing boats. The enterprise evolved into a home-improvement business after we saw the folly of spending our lives grubbing in oily bilges.

Molly worked at several odd (as in weird) jobs before re-entering the nursing field. One of them stands out sharply in my memory: She was hired by a fruit-packing company to demonstrate the correct method of slicing pineapples in the lobbies of Waikiki hotels. Each day she rode the bus across town in a long, flowing muumuu, carrying a large knife in a scabbard. After several frustrating months she managed to stumble through the labyrinth of the federal government's hiring procedures and landed a good nursing position at Tripler Army Hospital.

In 1987 we put *Swan* up for sale. Our business was thriving and we had lived aboard for 10 years. It seemed like the right thing to do. Sell the boat, buy a house, and forget the cruising life.

For several weeks we tolerated the brokers and potential buyers traipsing over the boat. I could hardly bear to look at the For Sale sign hanging from the lifeline. One morning, as I was leaving for work, I looked back at *Swan* lying in her slip—the sturdy little ship that had given Molly and I the best four years of our lives. I cut the sign down.

Hawaii is the crossroads of the North Pacific. Two slips away from us, our longtime friends from Portland, Kirk and Gladys Barnes, lived aboard their yacht *Scot Free*. A few slips beyond them was the yacht *Zingara*, owned by Jack and Donna Knapp, cruising comrades we had last seen in South Africa. It appeared that we were all hopelessly addicted to the sea and this special way of life.

When I learned that Jack and Donna were preparing *Zingara* to make their second circumnavigation I said, "Jack, come to your senses—there are big waves and everything out there." He knew, but he's incorrigible.

And now, after seven years of stocking the larder, we too are embarking on another open-ended voyage. This time our rough plan is to sail to Oregon for one more look at life on the river, then begin what will be, more or less, a circumnavigation of the United States.

The plans are not set in stone—that would ruin things. There's the recently created Tennessee-Tombigbee Waterway that opens the way to the inland river system and makes possible a boat ride through the country's heartland. It might provide an opportunity to realize a childhood dream of mine; a variation of a Huckleberry Finn drift down the Mississippi River, checking out the navigable tributaries along the way and sampling the spicy foods they prepare in Louisiana.

Daysailing up the Inland Waterway without being

bashed about seems like something we're ready for, and a sail on Chesapeake Bay—I know *Swan* wants to sail on Chesapeake Bay. A run up the Potomac river to check on Congress—one cannot check on Congress too often. Our plans are vague after that.

The mate has started the engine and *Swan* is trying to shake free. We're leaving as soon as I finish writing this sentence.

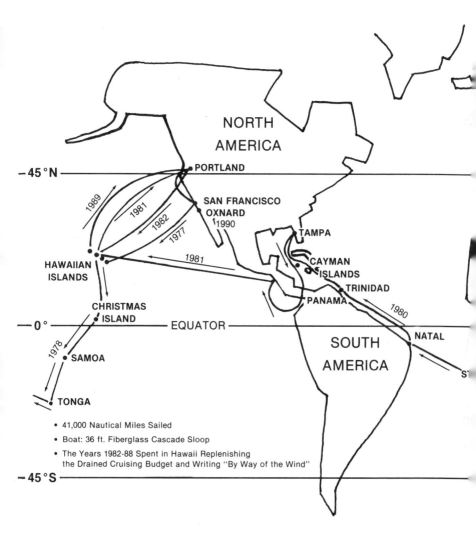

−45°N   PORTLAND

1989   1981   1982   1977

SAN FRANCISCO
OXNARD
1990

TAMPA

NORTH
AMERICA

1981

HAWAIIAN
ISLANDS

CAYMAN
ISLANDS
TRINIDAD

1980

CHRISTMAS
ISLAND

PANAMA

−0°   EQUATOR

1978

SAMOA

SOUTH
AMERICA

NATAL

S

TONGA

- 41,000 Nautical Miles Sailed
- Boat: 36 ft. Fiberglass Cascade Sloop
- The Years 1982-88 Spent in Hawaii Replenishing
  the Drained Cruising Budget and Writing "By Way of the Wind"

−45°S